# JANE EYRE ABRIDGED

Charlotte Brontë
Abridged by Cristina George
and Katherine Tarring

**Together we unlock every learner's unique potential**

At Hachette Learning (formerly Hodder Education), there's one thing we're certain about. No two students learn the same way. That's why our approach to teaching begins by recognising the needs of individuals first.

Our mission is to allow every learner to fulfil their unique potential by empowering those who teach them. From our expert teaching and learning resources to our digital educational tools that make learning easier and more accessible for all, we provide solutions designed to maximise the impact of learning for every teacher, parent and student.

Aligned to our parent company, Hachette Livre, founded in 1826, we pride ourselves on being a learning solutions provider with a global footprint.

www.hachettelearning.com

Although every effort has been made to ensure that website addresses are correct at time of going to press, Hachette Learning cannot be held responsible for the content of any website mentioned in this book. It is sometimes possible to find a relocated web page by typing in the address of the home page for a website in the URL window of your browser.

Hachette UK's policy is to use papers that are natural, renewable and recyclable products and made from wood grown in well-managed forests and other controlled sources. The logging and manufacturing processes are expected to conform to the environmental regulations of the country of origin.

To order, please visit www.HachetteLearning.com or contact Customer Service at education@hachette.co.uk / +44 (0)1235 827827.

ISBN: 978 1 0360 0416 7

© Charlotte Brontë. Abridged by Cristina George and Katherine Tarring 2025

First published in 2025 by
Hachette Learning,
An Hachette UK Company
Carmelite House
50 Victoria Embankment
London EC4Y 0DZ
www.HachetteLearning.com

The authorised representative in the EEA is Hachette Ireland, 8 Castlecourt Centre, Dublin 15, D15 XTP3, Ireland (email: info@hbgi.ie)

Impression number  10 9 8 7 6 5 4 3 2 1
Year                2029 2028 2027 2026 2025

All rights reserved. Apart from any use permitted under UK copyright law, no part of this publication may be reproduced or transmitted in any form or by any means, electronic or mechanical, including photocopying and recording, or held within any information storage and retrieval system, without permission in writing from the publisher or under licence from the Copyright Licensing Agency Limited. Further details of such licences (for reprographic reproduction) may be obtained from the Copyright Licensing Agency Limited, www.cla.co.uk

Cover photo: ©VectorStyle/Shutterstock
Typeset in the UK.
Printed in the UK.
A catalogue record for this title is available from the British Library.

# Reviews

*Jane Eyre* has been one of my 'desert island' books since I was young, so I was initially anxious when approaching this new version, wondering how George and Tarring could have done justice to Bronte's novel. I need not have worried. *Jane Eyre Abridged* manages that rare feat of being both faithful to the original and attractive to young readers. The gothic drama, the romance, the occasional humour and the feminism beloved of the original are all maintained, yet the shortened version is more immediately comprehensible. The authors have managed to maintain the measure and rhythm of the prose and retain challenging lexis, whilst weeding out the obscurer elements. Thus, *Jane Eyre Abridged* is a text that would inspire high-attaining students and, at the same time, be accessible to less confident readers. Furthermore, it does not patronise: the troubling aspects of the novel, such as the racist depictions of Bertha, are retained too, ripe for discussion and critique in a contemporary classroom.

I also appreciate the care has also been taken with the typesetting of the book, with a clear font and lines of dialogue clearly separated on the page – something that ensures the book would work well in an English lesson and would also encourage a casual reader to pick it up and feel immediately welcomed into the text.

*Dr Lorna Smith, Associate Professor in Education, University of Bristol*

Charlotte Brontë's *Jane Eyre* was the book that got me hooked into Literature. A teenage boy growing up in a Welsh coastal town identified with Jane's struggles and formation of her personality, confidence and strength. That's the power of good Literature: to connect the seemingly unconnected. So, it was with much pleasure that I read this version. A chance to open the door to this wonderful novel to students in KS3 or above.

Cristina George and Katherine Tarring have done the excellent job of condensing the novel without losing sight of the rich language and the complex themes. All the key elements are here yet accessible for the classroom. In addition to this, Cristina and Katherine have provided a wide range of interesting and appropriate resources to explore, challenge and investigate context, themes and ideas.

As a teacher who has taught Jane Eyre (well, parts of it) to Year 7 in the past, I wished I had this resource. They have done all the legwork for you, including key vocabulary, wider reading and so on. A fantastic resource for the department wanting to expand their repertoire of Literature texts in their curriculum and approach Literature from a female perspective: an area poorly served by the literary canon. Thankfully, we don't need a fire at Thornfield to adjust this imbalance. *Jane Eyre* and, more importantly, Charlotte Brontë rightfully deserve a stronger place in the English curriculum.

A well-thought out and planned resource which puts, in a meaningful and enjoyable way, Victorian Literature into English lessons.

Chris Curtis, Author and Head of English


This really is an excellent initiative – full of integrity – from two experienced and wise English subject leads. At a time when developing students' skills at KS3 can so often just mean extending the GCSE curriculum down a year or two, this project instead takes the approach that students deserve to be able to access the great literature of the past in a form that will help them to overcome some of the inevitable challenges involved. In recent years, studying the nineteenth century novel at KS3 has become increasingly difficult for both teachers and students. Text choices have often been made based solely on the length of a work – which is not always the most appropriate discriminator. *Jane Eyre* is a challenging novel – but an important one – and the editors' approach means that students can enjoy the scope and rhythm of the original, without any sense that they are being patronised by having the work 'translated' for them. The accompanying notes and resources are expertly pitched. They're uncluttered and have an eye to the overall cognitive load being experienced by students. In an age when students are so often bombarded with unhelpful 'knowledge', the activities provide excellent, extending contextual information and encourage students to get to the heart of what really matters in English – ie. thinking for themselves;

engaging in dialogue; developing a personal, critical response; and growing as a result of reading this great novel.

Chris Green, Head of English, Principal Examiner, Editor *(*The Use of English from the English Association*)*

What a brilliant resource! This is a thorough and comprehensive adaptation of *Jane Eyre* that is made readily accessible through its sympathetic reading and careful editing, losing none of the 'bite' of the original in the process. The accompanying resources are everything you'd need and more to bring this fabulous novel alive – all the work is done for you. By offering a fresh yet faithful perspective, and with its thoughtful approach and invaluable resources, this adaptation makes teaching *Jane Eyre* an absolute pleasure.

*Brian Ward, Head of English*

This thoughtful abridgement of *Jane Eyre* loses none of the richness, subtlety and nuances of the original classic. The authors have retained the authenticity of Bronte's voice, creating a version that allows immersion in the language and the tale's intricacies, without needing to allocate excessive curriculum time for studying the text. The chapter divisions have been carefully planned to ensure they can be completed in a lesson, alongside teaching activities to ensure comprehension and a deeper understanding of the novel's themes. Tailored to the abbreviated text and created to support the busy professional in the preparation and planning for teaching *Jane Eyre*, the authors have crafted interesting and engaging teaching resources, which are attractively presented and designed to foster the development of a range of skills that will benefit students in their study of literature: analysis, creative writing, vocabulary development and understanding how the context of a text affects its production and reception for contemporary and modern readers. They include astute learning questions which help steer the direction of study, linked to meticulously chosen themes. I thoroughly recommend both the text and its accompanying resources – a truly worthwhile investment!

*Olivia Williams, English Teacher and Head of Year*

This lovingly abridged edition of *Jane Eyre* strikes a perfect balance between accessibility and literary integrity, preserving the depth and complexity of Brontë's original work while making it more manageable for classroom study. The careful structuring of chapters ensures that each section can be meaningfully explored within a lesson, allowing students to engage with the novel's language, characters, and themes without feeling overwhelmed.

Accompanying the text is a set of thoughtfully designed resources that are both practical and purposeful. These materials not only support comprehension but also encourage analytical thinking, creative responses, and a deeper appreciation of the novel's historical and literary context. The activities are engaging, well-paced, and adaptable, making them a valuable asset for teachers navigating the demands of a busy curriculum.

For teachers looking to introduce *Jane Eyre* in a way that is both time-efficient and impactful, this abridged edition and its resources provide an excellent solution. Highly recommended!

*Tom Pollard, Assistant Head of English*

Following early careers leading fundraising for major arts institutions in London and organising special events from the family home near Salisbury, **Cristina George** gained her QTS in 2007. With more than 10 years' experience as Head of Department and a role as CPD and Training Lead, she believes that giving students access to works that move and inspire will forge a love of literature and introduced *Jane Eyre* to KS3 with this aim.

**Katherine Tarring** started her career in theatre, working as Casting Associate at the Royal Exchange Theatre, Manchester, before retraining as an English teacher. She now has 15 years' experience working in both independent and state schools. In her roles as Assistant Head of English and KS3 Coordinator, she has overseen the development of KS3 curricula, striving to ensure that students are challenged, engaged and inspired by English literature.

# Acknowledgements

Like all teachers, we have been influenced by the many wonderful practitioners who came before us and who generously share ideas in books, conversations, blogs and even in online chats. Although these resources are the culmination of many years of our teaching experience, we owe a debt to all those who helped shape our classroom practice and impacted our approach.

There are some individuals whom we would like to thank in particular: Charlotte Smallwood, Hugo Tarring, the wonderful Godolphin English team – past and present – Natasha Gladwell, Jessica Dunne and the team at John Catt/Hachette Learning.

Cristina George and Katherine Tarring

# Contents

Acknowledgements .................................................................. viii

Chapter 1 ................................................................................ 1

Chapter 2 ................................................................................ 5

Chapter 3 .............................................................................. 10

Chapter 4 .............................................................................. 14

Chapter 5 .............................................................................. 21

Chapter 6 .............................................................................. 27

Chapter 7 .............................................................................. 31

Chapter 8 .............................................................................. 35

Chapter 9 .............................................................................. 39

Chapter 10 ............................................................................ 43

Chapter 11 ............................................................................ 48

Chapter 12 ............................................................................ 55

Chapter 13 ............................................................................ 61

Chapter 14 ............................................................................ 68

Chapter 15 ............................................................................ 74

Chapter 16 ............................................................................ 81

Chapter 17 ............................................................................ 87

| | |
|---|---|
| Chapter 18 | 95 |
| Chapter 19 | 100 |
| Chapter 20 | 106 |
| Chapter 21 | 115 |
| Chapter 22 | 122 |
| Chapter 23 | 126 |
| Chapter 24 | 132 |
| Chapter 25 | 138 |
| Chapter 26 | 144 |
| Chapter 27 | 150 |
| Chapter 28 | 160 |
| Chapter 29 | 167 |
| Chapter 30 | 173 |
| Chapter 31 | 178 |
| Chapter 32 | 183 |
| Chapter 33 | 188 |
| Chapter 34 | 195 |
| Chapter 35 | 202 |
| Chapter 36 | 208 |
| Chapter 37 | 214 |
| Chapter 38 | 223 |

# Chapter 1

There was no possibility of taking a walk that day. We had been wandering in the leafless shrubbery an hour in the morning, but since dinner the cold winter wind had brought with it clouds so sombre and a rain so penetrating that further outdoor exercise was now out of the question.

I was glad of it. I never liked long walks, especially on chilly afternoons. Dreadful to me, was the coming home in the raw twilight with nipped fingers and toes, and a heart saddened by the scoldings of Bessie, the nurse, and humbled by my physical inferiority to Eliza, John, and Georgiana Reed.

Eliza, John, and Georgiana were now clustered round their mama in the drawing-room. She lay on a sofa by the fireside and, with her darlings about her, looked perfectly happy. Me, she had dispensed from joining the group, saying, "She regretted to be under the necessity of keeping me at a distance, but that until she could discover that I was endeavouring to be of a more sociable and childlike disposition and have a more attractive and sprightly manner, she really must exclude me from privileges intended only for contented, happy, little children."

"What does Bessie say I have done?" I asked.

"Jane, I don't like questioners. Besides, there is something truly forbidding in a child taking up her elders in that manner. Be seated somewhere, and until you can speak pleasantly, remain silent."

A breakfast-room adjoined the drawing-room. I slipped in there. It contained a bookcase. I soon possessed myself of a book, taking care that it should be one with pictures. I mounted the window-seat; gathering up my feet, I sat cross-legged and drew the curtain nearly close. Folds of scarlet drapery shut in my view to the right. To the left were the clear panes of glass, protecting, but not separating me from the November day. With the book on my knee, I was then happy – happy at least in my way. I feared nothing but interruption, and that came too soon. The breakfast-room door opened.

"Boh! Madam Mope!" cried the voice of John Reed. Then he paused; he found the room apparently empty.

"Where the dickens is she?" he continued. "Lizzy! Georgy! (calling to his sisters) Jane is not here. Tell mama she is run out into the rain – bad animal!"

"It is well I drew the curtain," thought I, and I wished fervently he might not discover my hiding-place, but Eliza put her head in at the door and said at once, "She is in the window-seat, to be sure, John."

And I came out immediately, for I trembled at the idea of being dragged forth.

"What do you want?" I asked, with awkward diffidence.

"Say, 'What do you want, Master Reed?'" was the answer. "I want you to come here," and seating himself in an armchair, he intimated by a gesture that I was to approach and stand before him.

John Reed was a schoolboy of fourteen years old: four years older than I – for I was but ten – large and stout for his age, with a dingy and unwholesome skin, heavy limbs and large extremities. He gorged himself habitually at table, which gave him a dim and bleared eye and flabby cheeks. He ought now to have been at school, but his mama had taken him home for a month or two, "on account of his delicate health."

John had not much affection for his mother and sisters, and he bullied and punished me, not two or three times in the week, nor once or twice in the day, but continually. Every nerve I had feared him and every morsel of flesh in my bones shrank when he came near.

Habitually obedient to John, I came up to his chair. I knew he would soon strike, and while dreading the blow, I mused on his disgusting and ugly appearance. I wonder if he read that notion in my face for, all at once,

# Chapter 1

without speaking, he struck suddenly and strongly. I tottered and retired back a step or two from his chair.

"That is for your impudence in answering mama," said he, "and for your sneaking way of getting behind curtains, and for the look you had in your eyes two minutes since, you rat!"

Accustomed to John Reed's abuse, I never had an idea of replying to it. My care was how to endure the blow which would certainly follow the insult.

"What were you doing behind the curtain?" he asked.

"I was reading."

"Show the book."

I returned to the window and fetched it.

"You have no business to take our books. You are a dependent, mama says. You have no money; your father left you none. You ought to beg, and not to live here with gentlemen's children like us, and eat the same meals we do, and wear clothes at our mama's expense. Go and stand by the door, out of the way of the mirror and the windows."

I did so, not at first aware what was his intention, but when I saw him lift and poise the book and stand in act to hurl it, I instinctively started aside with a cry of alarm. Not soon enough, however; the volume was flung. It hit me, and I fell, striking my head against the door and cutting it. The cut bled. The pain was sharp. My terror had passed its climax and other feelings succeeded.

"Wicked and cruel boy!" I said. "You are like a murderer – you are like a slave-driver!"

"What! What!" he cried. "Did she say that to me? Did you hear her, Eliza and Georgiana? I will tell mama, but first—"

He ran headlong at me. I felt him grasp my hair and my shoulder; he had closed with a desperate thing. I really saw in him a tyrant, a murderer. I felt a drop or two of blood from my head trickle down my neck and I retaliated frantically, not knowing what I did with my hands, but he called me "Rat! Rat!" and bellowed out aloud.

Aid was near. Eliza and Georgiana had run for Mrs Reed, who had gone upstairs. She now came upon the scene, followed by Bessie and her maid Abbot. We were parted. I heard the words –

"Dear! dear! What a fury to fly at Master John!"

"Did ever anybody see such a picture of passion!"

Then Mrs Reed subjoined –

"Take her away to the red-room, and lock her in there." Four hands were immediately laid upon me, and I was borne upstairs.

# Chapter 2

I resisted all the way, a new thing for me.

"Hold her arms, Miss Abbot: she's like a mad cat!" cried Bessie.

"For shame! for shame!" cried the lady's-maid. "What shocking conduct, Miss Eyre, to strike a young gentleman! Your young master."

"Master! How is he my master? Am I a servant?"

"No, you are less than a servant, for you do nothing for your keep. There, sit down, and think over your wickedness."

They had got me by this time into the apartment indicated by Mrs Reed and had thrust me upon a stool. My impulse was to rise from it like a spring, but their two pair of hands arrested me instantly.

"If you don't sit still, you must be tied down," said Bessie.

"Don't tie me down," I cried. "I will not stir."

"Mind you don't," said Bessie, and when she had ascertained that I was really subsiding, she loosened her hold of me; then she and Miss Abbot stood with folded arms, looking darkly and doubtfully on my face.

"You ought to be aware, Miss, that you have obligations to Mrs Reed: she keeps you; if she were to turn you out, you would have to go to the poorhouse."

I had nothing to say to these words: they were not new to me. This reproach of my dependence had become a vague sing-song in my ear: very painful and crushing, but only half intelligible. Miss Abbot joined in –

"And you ought not to think yourself on an equality with the Misses Reed and Master Reed, because Missis kindly allows you to be brought up with them. They will have a great deal of money and you will have none."

"What we tell you is for your good," added Bessie, in no harsh voice. "You should try to be useful and pleasant."

"Besides," said Miss Abbot, "God will punish her. Come, Bessie, we will leave her; I wouldn't have her heart for anything. Say your prayers, Miss Eyre."

They went, shutting the door, and locking it behind them.

The red-room was a square chamber, very seldom slept in, yet it was one of the largest and stateliest chambers in the mansion. A bed supported on massive pillars of mahogany, hung with curtains of deep-red damask, stood out in the centre; the two large windows, with their blinds always drawn down, were half shrouded in festoons and falls of similar drapery; the carpet was red; the table at the foot of the bed was covered with a crimson cloth; the walls were a soft fawn colour with a blush of pink in it; the wardrobe, the toilet-table, the chairs were of darkly polished old mahogany.

This room was chill, because it seldom had a fire; it was silent, because remote from the nursery and kitchen; solemn, because it was known to be so seldom entered. Only Mrs Reed herself, at far intervals, visited it to review the contents of a certain secret drawer in the wardrobe, where were stored her jewel-casket and a miniature of her deceased husband.

Mr Reed had been dead nine years; it was in this chamber he breathed his last.

I was not quite sure whether they had locked the door, and when I dared move, I got up and went to see. Alas! Yes: no jail was ever more secure.

Returning, I had to cross before the looking-glass; it revealed a strange little figure there gazing at me with a white face and arms specking the gloom, and glittering eyes of fear moving where all else was still. It had the effect of a real spirit; I thought it like one of the tiny phantoms Bessie's stories represented. I returned to my stool.

Superstition was with me at that moment; my blood was still warm. The mood of the revolted slave was still bracing me with its vigour.

All John Reed's violent tyrannies, all his sisters' proud indifference, all his mother's aversion, all the servants' partiality, turned up in my disturbed mind.

Why was I always suffering, always accused? Why could I never please? Why was it useless to try to win anyone's favour? Eliza, who was headstrong and selfish, was respected. Georgiana, who had a spoiled temper, was universally indulged. John, no one thwarted, much less punished, though he twisted the necks of the pigeons, set the dogs at the sheep and stripped the hothouse vines of their fruit. I dared commit no fault: I strove to fulfil every duty, and I was termed naughty and tiresome, sullen and sneaking, from morning to noon, and from noon to night.

My head still ached and bled with the blow and fall I had received, yet no one had reproved John for wantonly striking me.

"Unjust! Unjust!" said my reason.

I could not answer the ceaseless inward question – why I thus suffered.

Daylight began to forsake the red-room; it was past four o'clock and the beclouded afternoon was tending to drear twilight. I heard the rain still beating continuously on the staircase window, and the wind howling in the grove behind the hall. I grew by degrees cold as a stone and then my courage sank. My habitual mood of humiliation, self-doubt, depression, fell damp on the embers of my decaying ire.

All said I was wicked, and perhaps I might be so; what thought had I been but just conceiving of starving myself to death? That certainly was a crime, and was I fit to die and be laid in the vault under Gateshead Church? In such vault I had been told did Mr Reed lie buried, and led by this thought, I dwelt on it with gathering dread. I could not remember him, but I knew that he was my own uncle – my mother's brother – that he had taken me when a parentless infant to his house, and that in his last moments he had required a promise of Mrs Reed that she would rear and maintain me as one of her own children.

A singular notion dawned upon me. I doubted not that if Mr Reed had been alive he would have treated me kindly. Now, as I sat looking at the white bed and overshadowed walls, I began to recall what I had heard of dead men, troubled in their graves by the violation of their last wishes, revisiting the earth, and I thought Mr Reed's spirit might rise before me in this chamber.

I wiped my tears and hushed my sobs, fearful lest any sign of violent grief might waken a preternatural voice to comfort me. Shaking my hair from my eyes, I lifted my head and tried to look boldly round the dark room; at this moment a light gleamed on the wall.

Was it, I asked myself, a ray from the moon penetrating some aperture in the blind? No, moonlight was still, and this stirred; while I gazed, it glided up to the ceiling and quivered over my head. I can now conjecture that this streak of light was, in all likelihood, a gleam from a lantern carried by someone across the lawn, but then, prepared as my mind was for horror, shaken as my nerves were by agitation, I thought the swift darting beam was some vision from another world. My heart beat thick and my head grew hot; a sound filled my ears, which I deemed the rushing of wings; something seemed near me; I was oppressed, suffocated. I rushed to the door and shook the lock in desperate effort.

Steps came running along the outer passage; the key turned, and Bessie and Abbot entered.

"Miss Eyre, are you ill?" said Bessie.

"Take me out! Let me go into the nursery!" was my cry.

"What for? Are you hurt? Have you seen something?" again demanded Bessie.

"Oh! I saw a light and I thought a ghost would come." I had now got hold of Bessie's hand, and she did not snatch it from me.

"She has screamed out on purpose," declared Abbot, in disgust. "She only wanted to bring us all here. I know her naughty tricks."

"What is all this?" demanded another voice, and Mrs Reed came along the corridor, her cap flying wide, her gown rustling stormily. "Abbot and

# Chapter 2

Bessie, I believe I gave orders that Jane Eyre should be left in the red-room till I came to her myself."

"Miss Jane screamed so loud, ma'am," pleaded Bessie.

"Let her go," was the only answer. "Loose Bessie's hand, child. You will now stay here an hour longer and it is only on condition of perfect submission and stillness that I shall liberate you then."

"O aunt! Have pity! Forgive me! I cannot endure it – let me be punished some other way! I shall be killed if—"

"Silence! This violence is all most repulsive."

Mrs Reed abruptly thrust me back and locked me in. I heard her sweeping away and soon after she was gone. I suppose I had a sort of fit: unconsciousness closed the scene.

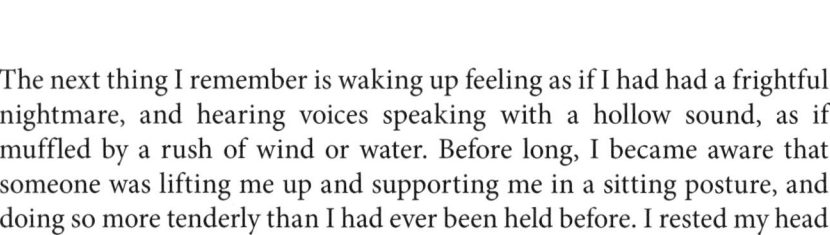

# Chapter 3

The next thing I remember is waking up feeling as if I had had a frightful nightmare, and hearing voices speaking with a hollow sound, as if muffled by a rush of wind or water. Before long, I became aware that someone was lifting me up and supporting me in a sitting posture, and doing so more tenderly than I had ever been held before. I rested my head against a pillow or an arm, and felt easy.

In five minutes more the cloud of bewilderment dissolved. I knew quite well that I was in my own bed, and that the red glare was the nursery fire. It was night; a candle burnt on the table. Bessie stood at the bed-foot with a basin in her hand, and a gentleman sat in a chair near my pillow, leaning over me.

I felt an inexpressible relief; I knew him. It was Dr Lloyd, who was sometimes called in by Mrs Reed when the servants were ailing. He charged Bessie to be very careful that I was not disturbed during the night and intimated that he should call again the next day. I felt so sheltered and befriended while he sat in the chair near my pillow, so that as he closed the door after him, all the room darkened and my heart again sank.

"Do you feel as if you should sleep, Miss?" asked Bessie, rather softly.

"I will try," I answered.

"Would you like to drink, or could you eat anything?"

"No, thank you, Bessie."

"Then I think I shall go to bed, for it is past twelve o'clock, but you may call me if you want anything in the night."

Wonderful kindness this! It emboldened me to ask a question.

# Chapter 3

"Bessie, what is the matter with me? Am I ill?"

"You fell sick, I suppose, in the red-room with crying. You'll be better soon, no doubt." Then she went next door where I heard her say:

"Sarah, come and sleep with me in the nursery. I daren't be alone with that poor child to-night. She might die. I wonder if she did see anything. Missis was rather too hard on her."

Sarah came back with Bessie and they both went to bed whispering together for half an hour before they fell asleep. For me, that long night passed in ghastly wakefulness. Ear, eye, and mind were strained by such dread as only children can feel.

No severe illness followed this; it only gave my nerves a shock. Next day, by noon, I was up and dressed, and sat wrapped in a shawl by the nursery hearth. I felt physically weak and broken down. This wretchedness kept drawing from me silent tears while all the time Bessie moved hither and thither putting away toys, addressing me now and then with a word of unexpected kindness. She had been down to the kitchen and brought up with her a tart on a brightly painted china plate. I was cordially invited to eat the delicate pastry. Vain favour! Coming, like most other favours often wished for, too late. I could not eat the tart. Bessie asked if I would have a book, but I put it on the table beside the untasted tart.

In the course of the morning Dr Lloyd came again.

"What, already up!" said he, as he entered the nursery. "Well, how is she?"

Bessie answered that I was doing very well.

"Then she ought to look more cheerful. I see you have been crying, Miss Jane Eyre. Can you tell me what about? Have you any pain?"

"No, sir."

"I daresay she is crying because she could not go out with Mrs Reed in the carriage," interposed Bessie.

"Surely not!"

I answered promptly, "I never cried for such a thing in my life. I hate going out in the carriage. I cry because I am miserable."

"Oh fie, Miss!" said Bessie.

The doctor appeared a little puzzled and fixed his eyes on me very steadily. Having considered me, he said:

"What made you ill yesterday?"

"I was knocked down," was the blunt explanation, jerked out of me by another pang of mortified pride, "but that did not make me ill," I added.

As I said this, a loud bell rang for the servants' dinner. "That's for you, nurse," said the doctor; "you can go down."

Bessie was obliged to go.

"The fall did not make you ill. What did, then?" pursued Dr Lloyd.

"I was shut up in a room where there is a ghost till after dark."

I saw Dr Lloyd smile and frown at the same time.

"Ghost! You are afraid of ghosts?"

"Of Mr Reed's ghost I am. He died in that room, and was laid out there. No one will go into it at night, if they can help it, and it was cruel to shut me up alone without a candle – so cruel that I shall never forget it."

"And is that what makes you so miserable? Are you afraid now in daylight?"

"No, but night will come again before long and besides, I am unhappy, very unhappy, for other things."

"What other things?"

How much I wished to reply fully to this question! How difficult it was to frame any answer! Fearful, however, of losing this only opportunity of relieving my grief, I tried to frame a brief though true response.

"I have no father or mother, brothers or sisters."

"You have a kind aunt and cousins."

"But John Reed knocked me down, and my aunt shut me up in the red-room."

# Chapter 3

"Are you not thankful to have such a fine place as Gateshead to live at?" he asked.

"If I had anywhere else to go, I should be glad to leave it."

"Have you any relations besides Mrs Reed?"

"I don't know. I asked Aunt Reed once, and she said possibly I might have some poor, low relations called Eyre, but she knew nothing about them."

"Would you like to go to school?"

I scarcely knew what school was. John Reed hated his school, and abused his master, but John Reed's tastes were no rule for mine, and Bessie's accounts of school, detailing certain accomplishments gained by young ladies, were attractive. Besides, school would be a complete change; it implied a long journey, an entire separation from Gateshead, an entrance into a new life.

"I should indeed like to go to school," was the audible conclusion of my musings.

"Well, well!" said Dr Lloyd, as he got up. "The child ought to have change of air and scene."

In the interview that followed between him and Mrs Reed, I presume Dr Lloyd recommended my being sent to school, and the recommendation was readily enough adopted, for as Abbot said, when I overheard her discussing the subject with Bessie, "Missis would be glad enough to get rid of such a tiresome child."

On that same occasion I also learned, for the first time, that my father had been a poor clergyman and that my mother had married him against the wishes of her friends, who considered the match beneath her. My grandfather Reed was so irritated at her disobedience that he cut her off without a shilling. And that after my mother and father had been married a year, the latter caught the typhus fever while visiting the poor, passing the infection to my mother so that both died within a month of each other.

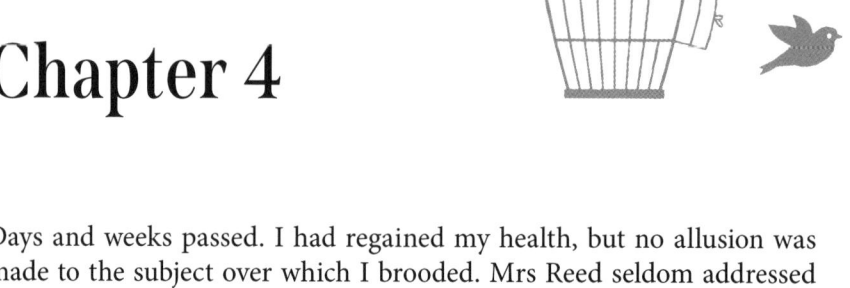

# Chapter 4

Days and weeks passed. I had regained my health, but no allusion was made to the subject over which I brooded. Mrs Reed seldom addressed me; since my illness, she had drawn a more marked line of separation between me and her own children, appointing me a small room to sleep in by myself, condemning me take my meals alone, and to pass all my time in the nursery, while my cousins were constantly in the drawing-room. Not a hint, however, did she drop about sending me to school. Still I felt that she would not long endure me under the same roof with her; for her glance, when turned on me, expressed an insuperable and rooted aversion.

Eliza and Georgiana, acting according to orders, spoke to me as little as possible. John thrust his tongue in his cheek whenever he saw me, but as I instantly turned against him, he ran from me to his mama.

"John: I told you – she is not worthy of notice. Do not you or your sisters associate with her."

Here, leaning over the banister, I cried out suddenly: "They are not fit to associate with me."

On hearing this audacious declaration, Mrs Reed ran nimbly up the stair, swept me like a whirlwind into the nursery, and dared me in an emphatic voice to rise from that place, or utter one syllable during the remainder of the day.

"What would Uncle Reed say to you, if he were alive?" was my demand, as if something spoke out of me over which I had no control.

"What?" said Mrs Reed under her breath with a look like fear, as if she really did not know whether I were child or fiend.

## Chapter 4

"My Uncle Reed is in heaven and can see all you do and think, and so can papa and mama. They know how you shut me up all day long, and how you wish me dead."

Mrs Reed shook me most soundly, boxed my ears, and then left me without a word. Bessie scolded me for an hour's length, in which she proved I was the most wicked child ever reared under a roof. I half believed her, for I felt indeed only bad feelings surging in my breast.

Christmas and the New Year had been celebrated at Gateshead with the usual festive cheer; presents had been interchanged, dinners and evening parties given. From every enjoyment I was, of course, excluded. My share of the gaiety consisted in witnessing Eliza and Georgiana descend to the drawing-room each evening, dressed in muslin frocks with scarlet sashes, and hair elaborately ringleted; in listening to the sound of the piano, to the jingling of glass and china as refreshments were handed; to the hum of conversation as the drawing-room door opened and closed. When tired of this occupation, I would retire from the stairhead to the solitary and silent nursery, somewhat sad.

Long did the hours seem while I waited for the sound of Bessie's step on the stairs. Sometimes she would bring me something by way of supper – a bun or a cheese-cake. She would sit on the bed while I ate it, and when I had finished, she would tuck the bed-clothes round me, and twice she kissed me, and said, "Good night, Miss Jane." When gentle like this, Bessie seemed to me the best, kindest being in the world, and I preferred her to anyone else at Gateshead Hall.

It was the fifteenth of January, about nine o'clock, when Bessie came running into the nursery. She hauled me to the washstand, inflicted a brief scrub on my face and hands with soap, water, and a coarse towel; disciplined my head with a bristly brush; denuded me of my pinafore, and then hurrying me to the top of the stairs, bid me go down directly, as I was wanted in the breakfast-room.

I slowly descended. For nearly three months, I had never been called to Mrs Reed's presence. Restricted so long to the nursery, the breakfast, dining, and drawing-rooms were become for me awful regions, on which it dismayed me to intrude. I now stood in the empty hall, before the breakfast-room door, intimidated and trembling. I feared to return to the nursery and feared to go forward to the parlour. Ten minutes I stood in agitated hesitation. The vehement ringing of the breakfast-room bell decided me. I must enter.

"Who could want me?" I asked inwardly, as with both hands I turned the stiff door-handle, which, for a second or two, resisted my efforts. "What should I see besides Aunt Reed in the apartment?" The handle turned, the door unclosed, and passing through and curtseying low, I looked up at – a black pillar! Such, at least, appeared to me, at first sight, the straight, narrow, sable-clad shape standing erect on the rug. The grim face at the top was like a carved mask.

Mrs Reed occupied her usual seat by the fireside; she signalled for me to approach and introduced me to the stony stranger with the words: "This is the little girl respecting whom I applied to you."

The man turned his head slowly towards me, and having examined me with inquisitive-looking grey eyes which twinkled under a pair of bushy brows, said solemnly, and in a bass voice, "Her size is small. How old is she?"

"Ten years."

"So much?" was the doubtful answer. "Your name, little girl?"

"Jane Eyre, sir."

"Well, Jane Eyre, and are you a good child?"

Impossible to reply in the affirmative; my little world held a contrary opinion. I was silent. Mrs Reed answered for me by an expressive shake of the head, adding, "Perhaps the less said on that subject the better, Mr Brocklehurst."

"Sorry to hear it!" He installed himself in the arm-chair opposite Mrs Reed's. "Come here," he said.

I stepped across the rug. He placed me square and straight before him. What a face he had! What a great nose! And what a mouth! And what large prominent teeth!

"Do you know," he began, "where the wicked go after death?"

# Chapter 4

"They go to hell," was my ready answer.

"And what is hell?"

"A pit full of fire."

"What must you do to avoid it?"

I deliberated before I replied: "I must keep in good health, and not die."

Mrs Reed interposed. "Mr Brocklehurst, I believe I intimated in the letter that this little girl has not quite the character and disposition I could wish. Should you admit her to Lowood school, I should be glad if the teachers were requested to keep a strict eye on her, and, above all, to guard against her worst fault, a tendency to deceit. I mention this in your hearing, Jane, so that you do not attempt to deceive Mr Brocklehurst."

Well might I dislike Mrs Reed, for it was her nature to wound me cruelly. However carefully I obeyed, however strenuously I strove to please her, my efforts were repulsed and repaid by such sentences as the above. Now, uttered before a stranger, the accusation cut me to the heart. I perceived that she was obliterating hope from this new phase of existence, sowing unkindness along my future path.

"Deceit is, indeed, a sad fault in a child," said Mr Brocklehurst. "She shall be watched, Mrs Reed. I will speak to Miss Temple and the teachers."

"I wish her to be brought up in a manner suiting her prospects," continued my aunt, "to be made useful, to be kept humble. As for the vacations, she will, with your permission, spend them always at Lowood."

"Consistency, madam, is the first of Christian duties observed in every arrangement connected with Lowood: plain fare, simple attire, unsophisticated accommodation, hardy and active habits; such as is the order of the day in the house and its inhabitants."

"I will send her, then, as soon as possible, Mr Brocklehurst. I feel anxious to be relieved of a responsibility that was becoming irksome."

With these words, Mr Brocklehurst, having rung for his carriage, departed.

Mrs Reed and I were left alone. Some minutes passed in silence; she was sewing, I was watching her. Mrs Reed looked up from her work.

"Return to the nursery," was her mandate.

I got up and went to the door; I came back again, close up to her.

Speak I must: "I am not deceitful. If I were, I should say I loved you; but I declare I do not love you: I dislike you the worst of anybody in the world except John Reed."

Mrs. Reed's hands still lay on her work, her eye of ice freezingly on mine.

"What more have you to say?" she asked, rather in the tone in which a person might address an opponent of adult age than a child.

"I am glad you are no relation of mine. I will never call you aunt again as long as I live. I will never come to see you when I am grown up, and if anyone asks me how I liked you, and how you treated me, I will say the very thought of you makes me sick, and that you treated me with miserable cruelty."

"How dare you affirm that, Jane Eyre?"

"How dare I, Mrs Reed? How dare I? Because it is the truth. You think I have no feelings, and that I can do without any bit of love or kindness, but I cannot. I shall remember how you thrust me back – roughly and violently – into the red-room, and locked me up there, to my dying day, though I was in agony, though I cried out, while suffocating with distress. And that punishment because your wicked boy struck me. I will tell anybody who asks me questions, this exact tale. People think you a good woman, but you are bad, hard-hearted. *You* are deceitful!"

Before I had finished, my soul began to expand, with the strangest sense of freedom, of triumph, I ever felt. It seemed as if an invisible bond had burst, and that I had struggled out into unhoped-for liberty. Mrs Reed looked frightened; her work had slipped from her knee; she was lifting up her hands, twisting her face as if she would cry.

"Jane, you don't understand these things. Children must be corrected for their faults."

"Deceit is not my fault!" I cried out in a savage, high voice.

## Chapter 4

"But you are passionate, Jane, and now return to the nursery – there's a dear – and lie down a little."

"I am not your dear. I cannot lie down. Send me to school soon, Mrs Reed, for I hate to live here."

"I will indeed send her to school soon," murmured Mrs Reed *sotto voce*, and gathering up her work, abruptly quitted the apartment.

I was left there alone – winner of the field. It was the hardest battle I had fought, and the first victory I had gained. I stood awhile on the rug, where Mr Brocklehurst had stood, and I enjoyed my conqueror's solitude. First, I smiled to myself and felt elate, but this fierce pleasure subsided in me as fast as the accelerated throb of my pulses. A child cannot quarrel with its elders, as I had done; cannot give its furious feelings uncontrolled play, as I had given mine, without experiencing afterwards the pang of remorse and the chill of reaction. A ridge of lighted heath, alive, glancing, devouring, would have been an appropriate emblem of my mind when I accused and menaced Mrs Reed. The same ridge, black and blasted after the flames are dead, would have represented as appropriately my subsequent condition, when half an hour's silence and reflection had shown me the madness of my conduct, and the dreariness of my hated and hating position.

Vengeance I had tasted for the first time; as aromatic wine it seemed, on swallowing, warm and racy. However, its after-flavour, metallic and corroding, gave me a sensation as if I had been poisoned. Willingly I would now have gone and asked Mrs Reed's pardon, but I knew, partly from experience and partly from instinct, that was the way to make her repulse me with double scorn, thereby re-exciting every raging impulse of my nature.

I took a book and endeavoured to read. I could make no sense of the subject. I went out to walk, but found no pleasure in the silent trees. I stood, a wretched child, whispering to myself over and over again, "What shall I do? What shall I do?"

All at once I heard a voice call, "Miss Jane! Come to lunch!"

It was Bessie, tripping down the path.

"You naughty little thing!" she said. "Why don't you come when you are called?"

I just put my two arms round her and said, "Come, Bessie! Don't scold."

Bessie stooped; we mutually embraced, and I followed her into the house comforted. That afternoon lapsed in peace and harmony. Even for me life had its gleams of sunshine.

# Chapter 5

Five o'clock had hardly struck on the morning of the 19th of January, when Bessie found me already up and nearly dressed. I was to leave Gateshead that day by a coach at six a.m. Bessie was the only person yet risen. She wrapped up some biscuits in a paper and put them into my bag. Then she and I left the nursery. As we passed Mrs Reed's bedroom, she said, "Will you go in and bid Missis good-bye?"

"No, Bessie. She came to my crib last night when you were gone down to supper, and said I need not disturb her in the morning, or my cousins either. She told me to remember that she had always been my best friend, and to speak of her and be grateful to her accordingly."

"What did you say, Miss?"

"Nothing. I covered my face with the bed-clothes, and turned from her to the wall."

"That was wrong, Miss Jane."

"It was quite right, Bessie. Your Missis has not been my friend. She has been my foe."

"O Miss Jane! Don't say so!"

"Good-bye to Gateshead!" cried I, as we passed through the hall and went out at the front door.

The moon was set, and it was very dark. Raw and chill was the winter morning: my teeth chattered as I hastened down the drive. There was a light in the porter's lodge; when we reached it, we found the porter's wife just kindling her fire.

"Is she going by herself?" asked the porter's wife. "Fifty miles is a long way! I wonder Mrs Reed is not afraid to trust her so far alone."

The coach drew up. There it was at the gates with its four horses and its top laden with passengers.

"Be sure and take good care of her," cried Bessie to the guard, as he lifted me into the inside.

"Ay, ay!" was the answer; the door was slapped to, a voice exclaimed, "All right," and on we drove. Thus was I severed from Bessie and Gateshead; thus whirled away to unknown, and, as I then deemed, remote and mysterious regions.

I remember but little of the journey. I only know that we appeared to travel over hundreds of miles of road. The afternoon came on wet and somewhat misty. As it waned into dusk, I began to feel that we were getting very far indeed from Gateshead. As twilight deepened, I heard a wild wind rushing amongst trees. Lulled by the sound, I at last dropped asleep and had not long slumbered when the coach-door was opened, and a person like a servant was standing at it.

"Is there a little girl called Jane Eyre here?" she asked. I answered "Yes," and was then lifted out. My trunk was handed down, and the coach instantly drove away.

I was stiff and bewildered. Gathering my faculties, I looked about me. Rain, wind, and darkness filled the air; nevertheless, I dimly discerned a door before me. Through this door I passed with my new guide and into a room with a fire, where she left me alone. I stood and warmed my numbed fingers over the blaze. Then the door opened, and an individual carrying a light entered; another followed close behind.

The first was a tall lady with dark hair, dark eyes, and a pale and large forehead.

"The child is very young to be sent alone," said she, putting her candle down on the table. She considered me attentively for a minute or two, then further added –

"She had better be put to bed soon; she looks tired. Are you tired?" she asked, placing her hand on my shoulder.

# Chapter 5

"A little, ma'am."

"And hungry too, no doubt. Let her have some supper before she goes to bed, Miss Miller."

Led by Miss Miller, I passed from passage to passage until we came upon the hum of many voices, and presently entered a wide, long room, in which were seated a congregation of girls of every age, from nine or ten to twenty. They were uniformly dressed in brown frocks and long pinafores.

Miss Miller signed to me to sit on a bench near the door, then walking up to the top of the long room she cried out –

"Monitors, fetch the supper-trays!"

The tall girls went out and returned, each bearing a tray, with portions of something arranged thereon, and a pitcher of water and mug in the middle of each tray. These were handed round, the mug being common to all. When it came to my turn, I drank, for I was thirsty, but did not touch the food. The meal over, prayers were read by Miss Miller, and the classes filed off, two and two, upstairs.

Overpowered by this time with weariness, I scarcely noticed what sort of a place the bedroom was. Tonight I was to be Miss Miller's bedfellow; she helped me to undress. When laid down I glanced at the long rows of beds, each of which was quickly filled with two occupants. In ten minutes the single light was extinguished, and amidst silence and complete darkness I fell asleep.

The night passed rapidly and when I again unclosed my eyes, a loud bell was ringing. The girls were up and dressing; day had not yet begun to dawn. I too rose reluctantly. It was bitter cold, and I dressed and washed as well as I could, though there was but one basin to six girls. Again the bell rang. All formed in file and entered the cold and dimly lit schoolroom. To Miss Miller's inferior class I was called, and placed at the bottom of it.

Business now began with a protracted reading of chapters in the Bible. The bell now sounded yet again. The classes were marshalled and marched into another room to breakfast: how glad I was to behold a prospect of getting something to eat!

The refectory was a great, low-ceiled, gloomy room. On two long tables smoked basins of something hot, which, however, to my dismay, sent forth an odour far from inviting. I saw a universal manifestation of discontent when the fumes of the repast met the nostrils of those destined to swallow it. From the tall girls of the first class, rose the whispered words:

"Disgusting! The porridge is burnt again!"

Ravenous, and now very faint, I devoured a spoonful or two of my portion without thinking of its taste, but then I perceived I had got in hand a nauseous mess. Burnt porridge is almost as bad as rotten potatoes. I saw each girl taste her food and try to swallow it, but in most cases the effort was soon relinquished.

Breakfast was over, and none had breakfasted. The refectory was evacuated for the schoolroom. Thereafter discipline prevailed and the classes were again seated, but all eyes were now turned to the woman who had received me last night. She surveyed the two rows of girls silently and gravely.

I retain yet the sense of admiring awe with which my eyes traced her steps. Seen now, in broad daylight, she looked tall, fair, and shapely with a stately air and carriage. This was Miss Temple, the superintendent of Lowood. Having taken her seat before a pair of globes placed on one of the tables, she summoned the first class round her, and commenced giving a lesson on geography. The duration of each lesson was measured by the clock, which at last struck twelve.

The superintendent rose.

"I have a word to address to the pupils," said she. "You had this morning a breakfast which you could not eat; you must be hungry. I have ordered that a lunch of bread and cheese shall be served to all."

The teachers looked at her with a sort of surprise.

"It is to be done on my responsibility," she added, in an explanatory tone to them, and immediately afterwards left the room.

# Chapter 5

The bread and cheese was presently brought in and distributed, to the high delight and refreshment of the whole school. The order was now given "To the garden!"

Outside, all was wintry blight and brown decay. I shuddered as I stood and looked round me. It was an inclement day for outdoor exercise. As yet I had spoken to no one, nor did anybody seem to take notice of me. I stood lonely enough, but to that feeling of isolation I was accustomed; it did not oppress me much. I looked round the garden, and then up at the house where a stone tablet over the door bore this inscription:

> LOWOOD INSTITUTION.
> This portion was rebuilt A.D. ——, by Naomi Brocklehurst, of Brocklehurst Hall, in this county.
> "Let your light so shine before men, that they may see your good works, and glorify your Father which is in heaven." – St. Matt. v. 16.

I was reading these words over and over again, when the sound of a cough close behind me made me turn my head. I saw a girl sitting on a stone bench near. She was bent over a book. In turning a leaf she happened to look up, and I said to her directly:

"Is your book interesting?" I had already formed the intention of asking her to lend it to me some day.

"I like it," she answered, after a pause of a second or two, during which she examined me.

"Can you tell me what the writing on that stone over the door means? What is Lowood Institution?"

"This house where you are come to live. It is partly a charity-school. You and I, and all the rest of us, are charity-children. I suppose you are an orphan. Are not either your father or your mother dead?"

"Both died before I can remember."

"Well, all the girls here have lost either one or both parents, and this is called an institution for educating orphans."

"Do we pay no money? Do they keep us for nothing?"

"We pay, or our friends pay, fifteen pounds a year for each."

"Then why do they call us charity-children?"

"Because fifteen pounds is not enough for board and teaching, and the deficiency is supplied by subscription."

"Who subscribes?"

"Different benevolent-minded ladies and gentlemen in this neighbourhood and in London."

"Does this house belong to that tall lady who said we were to have some bread and cheese?"

"To Miss Temple? Oh, no! I wish it did. She has to answer to Mr Brocklehurst for all she does. Mr Brocklehurst buys all our food and all our clothes."

"Have you been long here?"

"You ask rather too many questions. I have given you answers enough for the present. Now I want to read."

But at that moment the summons sounded for dinner; all re-entered the house. Thereafter, we immediately adjourned to the schoolroom where I saw the girl from the garden scolded by Miss Scatcherd, the history teacher, and sent to stand in the middle of the large schoolroom. The punishment seemed to me in a high degree ignominious, especially for so great a girl. But to my surprise she neither wept nor blushed; composed, she stood. "How can she bear it so quietly – so firmly?" I asked of myself. "Were I in her place, it seems to me I should wish the earth to open and swallow me up."

Soon after five p.m. we had another small meal. Half an hour's recreation succeeded, then study, then prayers and bed. Such was my first day at Lowood.

# Chapter 6

The next day commenced as before, getting up and dressing by rushlight, but this morning we were obliged to dispense with the ceremony of washing; the water in the pitchers was frozen. Breakfast-time came at last, and this morning the porridge was not burnt; the quality was eatable, the quantity small. How small my portion seemed! I wished it had been doubled.

In the course of the day I was enrolled a member of the fourth class. As I hemmed a piece of muslin, another class stood round Miss Scatcherd's chair, reading. It was English history. Among the readers I observed my acquaintance of the verandah. At the commencement of the lesson, her place had been at the top of the class, but for some error of pronunciation, or some inattention to stops, she was suddenly sent to the very bottom. Even in that obscure position, Miss Scatcherd continued to make her an object of constant notice. She was continually addressing to her such phrases as the following:

"Burns, you are standing on the side of your shoe; turn your toes out immediately." "Burns, you poke your chin most unpleasantly; draw it in." "Burns, I insist on your holding your head up. I will not have you before me in that attitude."

A chapter having been read through twice, the books were closed and the girls examined. The lesson had comprised part of the reign of Charles I, and there were sundry questions, which most of them appeared unable to answer. Still, every little difficulty was solved instantly when it reached Burns; her memory seemed to have retained the whole lesson, and she was ready with answers on every point. I kept expecting that Miss Scatcherd would praise her attention, but, instead of that, she suddenly cried out –

"You dirty, disagreeable girl! You have never cleaned your nails this morning!"

Burns made no answer. I wondered at her silence.

"Why," thought I, "does she not explain that she could neither clean her nails nor wash her face, as the water was frozen?"

My attention was now called off by Miss Smith desiring me to help her. When I returned to my seat, Burns immediately left the class, and going into the small inner room where the books were kept, returned in half a minute, carrying in her hand a bundle of twigs tied together at one end. This ominous tool she presented to Miss Scatcherd with a respectful curtesy. Then she quietly, and without being told, unloosed her pinafore, and the teacher instantly and sharply inflicted on her neck a dozen strokes with the bunch of twigs. Not a tear rose to Burns' eye and, while I paused from my sewing, because my fingers quivered at this spectacle with a sentiment of unavailing and impotent anger, not a feature of her pensive face altered its ordinary expression.

"Hardened girl!" exclaimed Miss Scatcherd. "Nothing can correct you of your slatternly habits. Carry the rod away."

Burns obeyed. I looked at her narrowly as she emerged from the book-closet. She was just putting back her handkerchief into her pocket, and the trace of a tear glistened on her thin cheek.

On that evening, I made my way to one of the fire-places. There I found Burns, absorbed, silent, in the companionship of a book, which she read by the dim glare of the embers. I sat down by her on the floor.

"What is your name besides Burns?"

"Helen."

"You must wish to leave Lowood?"

"No! Why should I? I was sent to Lowood to get an education, and it would be of no use going away until I have attained that object."

"But that teacher, Miss Scatcherd, is so cruel to you?"

"Cruel? Not at all! She is severe. She dislikes my faults."

## Chapter 6

"And if I were in your place I should dislike her; I should resist her. If she struck me with that rod, I should get it from her hand. I should break it under her nose."

"Probably you would do nothing of the sort, but if you did, Mr Brocklehurst would expel you from the school. That would be a great grief to your relations. It is far better to endure patiently a smart which nobody feels but yourself, than to commit a hasty action, and besides, the Bible bids us return good for evil."

"But then it seems disgraceful to be flogged, and to be sent to stand in the middle of a room full of people. I could not bear it."

"Yet it would be your duty to bear it."

I heard her with wonder: I could not comprehend this doctrine of endurance. Still, I felt that Helen Burns might be right and I wrong.

"You say you have faults, Helen. What are they? To me you seem very good."

"I seldom put, and never keep, things in order. I am careless. I forget rules. I read when I should learn my lessons. This is all very provoking to Miss Scatcherd, who is naturally neat, punctual, and particular."

"And cross and cruel," I added, but Helen Burns would not admit my addition. She kept silence.

"Is Miss Temple as severe to you as Miss Scatcherd?"

At the utterance of Miss Temple's name, a soft smile flitted over her grave face.

"Miss Temple is full of goodness. It pains her to be severe to anyone, even the worst in the school. She sees my errors, and tells me of them gently and, if I do anything worthy of praise, she gives it liberally."

"I feel, Helen, that I must dislike those who, whatever I do to please them, persist in disliking me. I must resist those who punish me unjustly. It is as natural as that I should love those who show me affection, or submit to punishment when I feel it is deserved."

"Read the New Testament, and observe what Christ says, and how He acts. Make His word your rule, and His conduct your example."

"What does He say?"

"Love your enemies; bless them that curse you; do good to them that hate you and despitefully use you."

"Then I should love Mrs Reed, which I cannot do. I should bless her son John, which is impossible."

In her turn, Helen Burns asked me to explain, and I proceeded forthwith to pour out, in my own way, the tale of my sufferings and resentments. Bitter and truculent when excited, I spoke as I felt, without reserve or softening.

Helen heard me patiently to the end. I expected she would then make a remark, but she said nothing.

"Well," I asked impatiently, "is not Mrs Reed a hard-hearted, bad woman?"

"She has been unkind to you, no doubt, but how minutely you remember all she has done and said to you! Would you not be happier if you tried to forget her severity? Life appears to me too short to be spent in nursing animosity or registering wrongs. We are, and must be, one and all, burdened with faults in this world, but the time will soon come when sin will fall from us, and only the spirit will remain. I live in calm, looking to the end."

I saw by her look she wished no longer to talk to me. She was not allowed much time for meditation. A monitor presently came up, exclaiming –

"Helen Burns, if you don't go and put your drawer in order, and fold up your work this minute, I'll tell Miss Scatcherd to come and look at it!"

Helen sighed as her reverie fled, and getting up, obeyed the monitor without reply as without delay.

# Chapter 7

My first quarter at Lowood seemed an age. During January, February, and part of March, the deep snows prevented our stirring beyond the garden walls, but within these limits we had to pass an hour every day in the open air. Our clothing was insufficient to protect us from the severe cold. We had no boots, so the snow got into our shoes and melted there; our ungloved hands became numbed, as were our feet. Then the scanty supply of food was distressing; we had scarcely sufficient to keep alive a delicate invalid. From this deficiency of nourishment resulted an abuse: whenever the famished great girls had an opportunity, they would coax or menace the little ones out of their portion.

One afternoon (I had then been three weeks at Lowood), as I was sitting with a slate in my hand, puzzling over a sum, my eyes caught sight of a figure just passing. A long stride measured the schoolroom, and presently beside Miss Temple, who herself had risen, stood the same black column which had frowned on me so ominously from the hearthrug of Gateshead. It was Mr Brocklehurst, looking longer, narrower, and more rigid than ever.

Too well I remembered the hints given by Mrs Reed about my character, the promise pledged by Mr Brocklehurst to apprise the teachers of my vicious nature. All along I had been dreading the fulfilment of this promise – I had been looking out daily for the man whose information respecting my past life was to brand me as a bad child for ever: now there he was.

He stood at Miss Temple's side, and I caught most of what he said.

"Miss Temple, you may tell Miss Smith that she is not, on any account, to give out more than one needle at a time to each pupil. If they have more, they are apt to be careless and lose them."

"Your directions shall be attended to, sir," said Miss Temple.

"And, ma'am," he continued, "I find, in settling accounts with the housekeeper, that a lunch, consisting of bread and cheese, has twice been served out to the girls during the past fortnight. Who introduced this innovation? And by what authority?"

"I must be responsible for the circumstance, sir," replied Miss Temple. "The breakfast was so ill prepared that the pupils could not possibly eat it, and I dared not allow them to remain fasting till dinner-time."

"Madam, allow me an instant. You are aware that my plan in bringing up these girls is not to accustom them to habits of luxury and indulgence, but to render them patient and self-denying. An instructor should take the opportunity of referring to our blessed Lord himself: 'If ye suffer hunger or thirst for My sake, happy are ye.' Oh, madam, when you put bread and cheese, instead of burnt porridge, into these children's mouths, you may indeed feed their vile bodies, but you little think how you starve their immortal souls!"

Mr Brocklehurst again paused – perhaps overcome by his feelings. Miss Temple had looked down when he first began to speak to her, but she now gazed straight before her, and her face, naturally pale as marble, appeared to be assuming the coldness and fixity of that material.

Meantime, Mr Brocklehurst, standing on the hearth with his hands behind his back, majestically surveyed the whole school. Suddenly his eye gave a blink.

Turning, he said, "Miss Temple, Miss Temple, what – what is that girl with curled hair? Red hair, ma'am, curled – curled all over?" And extending his cane he pointed to the awful object, his hand shaking as he did so.

"It is Julia Severn," replied Miss Temple, very quietly.

"Julia Severn, ma'am! And why has she, or any other, curled hair?"

"Julia's hair curls naturally," returned Miss Temple, still more quietly.

"Naturally! Yes, but we are not to conform to nature. And why that abundance? Miss Temple, that girl's hair must be cut off entirely; I will send a barber to-morrow. Tell all the first form to rise up and direct their faces to the wall."

## Chapter 7

He scrutinised the reverse of these living medals some five minutes, then pronounced sentence.

"All those top-knots must be cut off."

Miss Temple seemed to remonstrate.

"Madam," he pursued, "I have a Master to serve whose kingdom is not of this world. My mission is to teach these girls to clothe themselves with shame-facedness and sobriety, not with braided hair and—"

Mr Brocklehurst was here interrupted; three other visitors, ladies, now entered the room splendidly attired in velvet, silk, and furs. The two younger of the trio (fine girls of sixteen and seventeen) had grey beaver hats with ostrich plumes, and from under the brim fell a profusion of light tresses, elaborately curled.

These ladies were deferentially received by Miss Temple, as Mrs and the Misses Brocklehurst, and conducted to seats of honour at the top of the room.

I had sat well back on the form, and while seeming to be busy with my sum, had held my slate in such a manner as to conceal my face. I might have escaped notice, had not my treacherous slate somehow happened to slip from my hand, and falling with an obtrusive crash, directly drawn every eye upon me. I knew it was all over now, and, as I stooped to pick up the two fragments of slate, I rallied my forces for the worst. It came.

"A careless girl!" said Mr Brocklehurst, and immediately after: "It is the new pupil, I perceive." And before I could draw breath, "Let the child who broke her slate come forward!"

Of my own accord I could not have stirred. I was paralysed, but Miss Temple gently assisted me, and I caught her whispered counsel: "Don't be afraid, Jane, I saw it was an accident; you shall not be punished."

The kind whisper went to my heart like a dagger. An impulse of fury against Brocklehurst bounded in my pulses. I was no Helen Burns.

"Fetch that stool," said Mr Brocklehurst, pointing to a very high one from which a monitor had just risen. It was brought.

"Place the child upon it."

And I was placed there, by whom I don't know. I was only aware that they had hoisted me up to the height of Mr Brocklehurst's nose, and that he was within a yard of me.

"Ladies," said he, turning to his family, "Miss Temple, teachers, and children, you all see this girl? You see she is yet young; who would think that the Evil One had already found a servant and agent in her? Yet such, I grieve to say, is the case."

A pause – in which I began to feel that the trial, no longer to be shirked, must be firmly sustained.

"My dear children," pursued the black marble clergyman, "it becomes my duty to warn you – you must be on your guard against this girl. You must avoid her company, exclude her from your sports, and shut her out from your converse. Teachers, you must watch her. Weigh well her words, punish her body to save her soul, if, indeed, such salvation be possible, for (my tongue falters while I tell it) this child, this girl is – a liar!"

I observed all the female Brocklehursts produce their pocket-handkerchiefs, while the elderly lady swayed herself to and fro, and the two younger ones whispered, "How shocking!"

Mr Brocklehurst resumed.

"This I learned from the charitable lady who adopted her in her orphan state, reared her as her own daughter, and whose kindness, whose generosity, the unhappy girl repaid by a dreadful ingratitude. She has sent her here to be healed."

Mr Brocklehurst adjusted his top button and, turning at the door, said –

"Let her stand half an hour longer on that stool, and let no one speak to her during the remainder of the day."

There was I, then, mounted aloft. What my sensations were, no language can describe, but just as they all rose, stifling my breath and constricting my throat, Helen Burns came up and passed me. In passing, she lifted her eyes. What a strange light inspired them! How the new feeling bore me up! I mastered the rising hysteria, lifted up my head, and took a firm stand on the stool.

# Chapter 8

Ere the half-hour ended, and five o'clock struck; school was dismissed, and all were gone to tea. I now ventured to descend; it was deep dusk. I retired into a corner and sank to the ground. I wept: Helen Burns was not here; nothing sustained me; left to myself, I abandoned myself, and my tears watered the boards.

I had meant to be so good, and to do so much at Lowood; to make so many friends, to earn respect and win affection. Already I had made visible progress: that very morning I had reached the head of my class and I was well received by my fellow-pupils. Now, here I lay again crushed and trodden on, and could I ever rise more?

While I was sobbing, someone approached: I started up – again Helen Burns was near me; she brought my coffee and bread.

"Come, eat something," she said, but I put both away from me; though I tried hard, I continued to weep aloud. She sat down on the ground near me and remained silent. I was the first who spoke –

"Helen, why do you stay with a girl whom everybody believes to be a liar?"

"Everybody, Jane? Why, there are only eighty people who have heard you called so, and the world contains hundreds of millions."

"But what have I to do with millions? The eighty, I know, despise me."

"Jane, you are mistaken: probably not one in the school either despises or dislikes you; many, I am sure, pity you much."

"How can they pity me after what Mr Brocklehurst has said?"

"Mr Brocklehurst is not a god, nor is he even a great and admired man; he is little liked here. Besides, Jane, if all the world hated you, and believed you wicked, while your own conscience approved you, and absolved you from guilt, you would not be without friends."

"No, I know I should think well of myself, but that is not enough: if others don't love me I would rather die than live – I cannot bear to be solitary and hated, Helen."

"Hush, Jane! You think too much of the love of human beings; you are too impulsive. God waits only the separation of spirit from flesh to crown us with a full reward. Why, then, should we ever sink overwhelmed with distress, when life is so soon over, and death is so certain an entrance to happiness – to glory?"

I was silent and when, having done speaking, she breathed a little fast and coughed a short cough, I momentarily forgot my own sorrows to yield to a vague concern for her.

Resting my head on Helen's shoulder, I put my arms round her waist; she drew me to her, and we reposed in silence. We had not sat long thus, when another person came in which we at once recognised as Miss Temple.

"I came on purpose to find you, Jane Eyre," said she. "I want you in my room and as Helen Burns is with you, she may come too."

Her apartment contained a good fire, and looked cheerful. Miss Temple told Helen Burns to be seated in a low arm-chair on one side of the hearth, and herself taking another, she called me to her side.

"Is it all over?" she asked, looking down at my face. "Have you cried your grief away?"

"I am afraid I never shall do that."

"Why?"

"Because I have been wrongly accused and you, ma'am, and everybody else, will now think me wicked."

"We shall think you what you prove yourself to be, my child. Continue to act as a good girl, and you will satisfy us. Jane, you know that when a criminal is accused, he is always allowed to speak in his own defence.

## Chapter 8

You have been charged with falsehood; defend yourself to me as well as you can. Say whatever your memory suggests is true, but add nothing and exaggerate nothing."

I resolved, in the depth of my heart, that I would be most moderate – most correct and, having reflected a few minutes, I told her all the story of my sad childhood and felt as I went on that Miss Temple fully believed me.

In the course of the tale I had mentioned Dr Lloyd as having come to see me after the fit. Miss Temple regarded me a few minutes in silence. She then said –

"I know something of Dr Lloyd. I shall write to him; if his reply agrees with your statement, you shall be publicly cleared from every imputation; to me, Jane, you are clear now."

She kissed me, and still keeping me at her side, she proceeded to address Helen Burns.

"How are you to-night, Helen? Have you coughed much to-day?"

"Not quite so much, I think, ma'am."

"And the pain in your chest?"

"It is a little better."

Miss Temple got up, took her hand and examined her pulse, then she returned to her own seat; as she resumed it, I heard her sigh low. She was pensive a few minutes, then rousing herself, she said cheerfully –

"But you two are my visitors to-night; I must treat you as such." She rang her bell.

"Barbara," she said to the servant who answered it, "I have not yet had tea; bring the tray and place cups for these two young ladies."

And a tray was soon brought. How pretty, to my eyes, did the china cups and bright teapot look, placed on the little round table near the fire! How fragrant was the steam of the beverage, and the scent of the toast!

Having invited Helen and me to approach the table, and placed before each of us a cup of tea with one delicious but thin morsel of toast, she

37

got up, unlocked a drawer, and taking from it a parcel wrapped in paper, disclosed presently to our eyes a good-sized seed-cake and proceeded to cut slices with a generous hand.

We feasted that evening and, tea over and the tray removed, Miss Temple again summoned us to the fire; we sat one on each side of her, and now a conversation followed between her and Helen, which it was indeed a privilege to be admitted to hear.

They conversed of things I had never heard of; of nations and times past; of countries far away; they spoke of books: how many they had read! What stores of knowledge they possessed! They had scarcely finished ere the bell announced bedtime. Miss Temple embraced us both, saying, as she drew us to her heart –

"God bless you, my children!"

Helen she held a little longer than me: she let her go more reluctantly; it was Helen her eye followed to the door; it was for her she a second time breathed a sad sigh; for her she wiped a tear from her cheek.

On reaching the bedroom, we heard the voice of Miss Scatcherd: she was examining drawers. She had just pulled out Helen Burns's, and when we entered Helen was greeted with a sharp reprimand, and told that to-morrow she should have half a dozen of untidily folded articles pinned to her shoulder.

About a week subsequently to the incidents above narrated, Miss Temple, who had written to Dr Lloyd, received his answer: it appeared that what he said went to corroborate my account. Miss Temple, having assembled the whole school, announced that inquiry had been made into the charges alleged against Jane Eyre, and that she was most happy to be able to pronounce her completely cleared from every imputation. The teachers then shook hands with me and kissed me, and a murmur of pleasure ran through the ranks of my companions.

Thus relieved of a grievous load, I from that hour set to work afresh, resolved to pioneer my way through every difficulty.

# Chapter 9

The hardships of Lowood lessened. Spring drew on; the frosts of winter had ceased; its snows were melted, its cutting winds ameliorated. My wretched feet, swollen to lameness by the sharp air of January, began to heal and subside under the gentler breathings of April.

April advanced to May: days of blue sky and placid sunshine. And now vegetation matured with vigour; Lowood shook loose its tresses; it became all green, all flowery. Assuredly, it was pleasant enough, but whether healthy or not is another question.

That forest-dell, where Lowood lay, was the cradle of fog and fog-bred pestilence. It crept into the Orphan Asylum, breathed typhus through its crowded schoolroom and dormitory, and, ere May arrived, transformed the seminary into an hospital.

Semi-starvation and neglected colds had predisposed most of the pupils to receive infection: forty-five out of the eighty girls lay ill at one time. Classes were broken up, rules relaxed. Miss Temple's whole attention was absorbed by the patients: she lived in the sick-room, never quitting it except to snatch a few hours' rest at night. Some died at the school, and were buried quietly and quickly.

But I, and the rest who continued well, enjoyed fully the beauties of the scene and season; we did what we liked, went where we liked; we lived better too. Mr Brocklehurst and his family never came near Lowood now. There were fewer to feed; the sick could eat little; our breakfast-basins were better filled.

And why did I not spend these sweet days of liberty with Helen? Had I forgotten her?

She was ill at present: for some weeks she had been removed from my sight to I knew not what room upstairs. Her complaint was consumption, not typhus, which I wrongly understood as something mild, which time and care would be sure to alleviate.

One evening, in the beginning of June, I had stayed out very late and when I got back, it was after moonrise: the flowers smelt so sweet as the dew fell; it was such a pleasant evening, so serene, so warm. I was noting these things and enjoying them as a child might, when it entered my mind as it had never done before –

"How sad to be lying now on a sick bed, and to be in danger of dying!"

And then my mind made its first earnest effort to comprehend what had been infused into it concerning heaven and hell, and for the first time it recoiled, baffled. While pondering this new idea, I heard the front door open and the nurse come out.

"How is Helen Burns?" I asked her.

"Very poorly," was her answer.

"And what does the doctor say about her?"

"He says she'll not be here long."

It opened clear on my comprehension that Helen Burns was numbering her last days in this world. I experienced a shock of horror, then a strong thrill of grief, then a desire – a necessity – to see her, and I asked in what room she lay.

"She is in Miss Temple's room," said the nurse.

"May I go up and speak to her?"

"Oh no, child!"

The nurse closed the front door. I went in by the side entrance where Miss Miller was calling the pupils to go to bed.

It might be two hours later, probably near eleven, when I rose softly, put on my frock over my night-dress, and, without shoes, crept from the apartment, and set off in quest of Miss Temple's room. It was quite at the other end of the house, but I knew my way. I dreaded being discovered and sent back; for I must see Helen – I must embrace her before she died – I must give her one last kiss, exchange with her one last word.

Having descended a staircase, traversed a portion of the house below, and succeeded in opening and shutting, without noise, two doors, I reached another flight of steps; these I mounted, and then just opposite to me was Miss Temple's room. Close by Miss Temple's bed, and half covered with its white curtains, there stood a little crib.

"Helen!" I whispered softly, "are you awake?"

She stirred herself, put back the curtain, and I saw her face: pale, wasted, but quite composed.

"Can it be you, Jane?" she asked, in her own gentle voice.

"Oh!" I thought, "she is not going to die; they are mistaken: she could not speak and look so calmly if she were."

I got on to her crib and kissed her. Her forehead was cold, and her cheek both cold and thin, and so were her hand and wrist but she smiled as of old.

"Why are you come here, Jane? It is past eleven o'clock."

"I came to see you, Helen: I heard you were very ill, and I could not sleep till I had spoken to you."

"You came to bid me good-bye, then; you are just in time probably."

"Are you going somewhere, Helen? Are you going home?"

"Yes; to my long home – my last home."

"No, no, Helen!" I stopped, distressed. While I tried to devour my tears, a fit of coughing seized Helen; when it was over, she lay some minutes exhausted; then she whispered –

"Jane, your little feet are bare; lie down and cover yourself with my quilt."

I did so: she put her arm over me, and I nestled close to her. After a long silence, she resumed, still whispering –

"I am very happy, Jane, and when you hear that I am dead, you must be sure and not grieve: there is nothing to grieve about. We all must die one day, and by dying young, I shall escape great sufferings."

"But where are you going to, Helen? Can you see? Do you know?"

"I believe; I have faith: I am going to God."

"And shall I see you again, Helen, when I die?"

"You will come to the same region of happiness; be received by the same mighty, universal Parent, no doubt, dear Jane."

I clasped my arms closer round Helen. She seemed dearer to me than ever. I felt as if I could not let her go; I lay with my face hidden on her neck. Presently she said, in the sweetest tone –

"How comfortable I am! But don't leave me, Jane; I like to have you near me."

"I'll stay with you, dear Helen: no one shall take me away."

"Are you warm, darling?"

"Yes."

"Good-night, Jane."

"Good-night, Helen."

She kissed me, and I her, and we both soon slumbered.

When I awoke it was day; an unusual movement roused me. I looked up; I was in somebody's arms, and the nurse was carrying me through the passage back to the dormitory. I was not reprimanded for leaving my bed; no explanation was afforded then to my many questions, but a day or two afterwards I learned that Miss Temple, on returning to her own room at dawn, had found me laid in the little crib, my face against Helen Burns's shoulder, my arms round her neck. I was asleep, and Helen was – dead.

Her grave is in Brocklebridge churchyard. For fifteen years after her death it was only covered by a grassy mound, but now a grey marble tablet marks the spot, inscribed with her name, and the word "*Resurgam.*"

# Chapter 10

When the typhus fever had fulfilled its mission of devastation at Lowood, it gradually disappeared but the number of its victims had drawn public attention on the school. Inquiry was made and various facts came out which excited public indignation. The unhealthy nature of the site; the quantity and quality of the children's food; the pupils' wretched clothing and accommodations – all these things were discovered.

Several wealthy and benevolent individuals in the county subscribed for the erection of a more convenient building; new regulations were made; improvements in diet and clothing introduced. The school, thus improved, became in time a truly useful and noble institution. I remained an inmate of its walls, after its regeneration, for eight years: six as pupil, and two as teacher.

During these eight years I had the means of an excellent education placed within my reach; I availed myself fully of the advantages offered me. In time I rose to be the first girl of the first class; then I was invested with the office of teacher, which I discharged with zeal for two years, but at the end of that time I altered.

Miss Temple's friendship and society had been my continual solace; she had stood me in the stead of mother, governess, and, latterly, companion. At this period she married, removed with her husband to a distant county, and consequently was lost to me.

From the day she left I was no longer the same: with her was gone every association that had made Lowood in some degree a home to me. My world had for some years been in Lowood: my experience had been of its rules and systems; now I remembered that the real world was wide, and that a variety of sensations and excitements awaited those who had courage to go forth into its expanse.

I walked about the chamber most of the time, regretting my loss, and thinking how to repair it. I looked up and found that the afternoon was gone, and evening far advanced. I went to my window, opened it, and looked out. There were the two wings of the Lowood; there was the garden; there was the hilly horizon. My eye passed all other objects to rest on those most remote: the blue peaks. It was those I longed to surmount; all within their boundary seemed prison-ground. I traced the white road winding round the base of one mountain. How I longed to follow it farther! School-rules, school-duties, school-habits – such was what I knew of existence. And now I felt that it was not enough. I desired liberty; for liberty I gasped. I proceeded to think with all my might.

"What do I want? A new place, in a new house, amongst new faces, under new circumstances. How do people do to get a new place? They apply to friends, I suppose: I have no friends." I took a turn in the room and crept to bed.

As I lay down, it came quietly and naturally to my mind: "You must advertise in the ——*shire Herald*."

With the earliest day, I was up; I had my advertisement written –

*"A young lady accustomed to tuition is desirous of meeting with a situation in a private family. She is qualified to teach the usual branches of a good English education, together with French, Drawing, and Music. Address: J.E., Post-office, Lowton."*

This document remained locked in my drawer all day. After tea, I asked leave to go to Lowton. It was a walk of two miles, but the days were still long; I slipped the letter into the post-office, and came back with a relieved heart.

The succeeding week seemed long. It came to an end at last, and once more I found myself afoot on the road to Lowton. I stepped across the clean and quiet little street to the post-office: it was kept by an old dame, who wore horn spectacles on her nose, and black mittens on her hands.

"Are there any letters for J.E.?" I asked.

## Chapter 10

She peered at me over her spectacles, and then she opened a drawer and fumbled among its contents for a long time, so long that my hopes began to falter. At last she presented a document across the counter.

"Is there only one?" I demanded.

"There are no more," said she.

The contents of the letter were brief.

*"If J.E., who advertised in the ——shire Herald of last Thursday, is in a position to give satisfactory references as to character and competency, a situation can be offered her where there is but one pupil, a little girl, under ten years of age; and where the salary is thirty pounds per annum. J.E. is requested to send references, and all particulars, to the direction: 'Mrs Fairfax, Thornfield, near Millcote.'"*

I examined the document long: the writing was old-fashioned and rather uncertain, like that of an elderly lady. Mrs Fairfax! I saw her in a black gown and widow's cap. Thornfield! That, doubtless, was the name of her house.

Next day new steps were to be taken; I must impart my plans in order to achieve their success. Having sought and obtained a testimonial of character and capacity, signed by the inspectors of Lowood, I forwarded a copy of it to Mrs Fairfax and got that lady's reply, stating that she was satisfied, and fixing that day fortnight as the period for my assuming the post of governess in her house.

I now busied myself in preparations. I had not a very large wardrobe, though it was adequate, and the last day sufficed to pack my trunk – the same I had brought with me eight years ago from Gateshead. I had brushed my black travelling-dress, prepared my bonnet, gloves, and muff. A phase of my life was closing, a new one opening.

"Miss," said a servant who met me in the lobby, "a person below wishes to see you."

I ran downstairs without inquiry. I saw a woman attired like a well-dressed servant, very good-looking, with black hair and eyes, and lively complexion.

"You've not quite forgotten me, I think, Miss Jane?" she asked, in a voice and with a smile I half recognised.

In another second I was embracing and kissing her rapturously. "Bessie!" I said, whereat she half laughed, half cried, and we both went into the parlour.

"Well, and how do they all get on at Gateshead?" I asked.

"Georgiana and her sister are always quarrelling—"

"What of John Reed?"

"Oh, he is not doing so well as his mama could wish. He went to college, but he is such a dissipated young man they will never make much of him, I think. He spends a deal of money."

"I am afraid you are disappointed in me, Bessie." I said this laughing.

"No, Miss Jane, not exactly: you were no beauty as a child."

I smiled at Bessie's frank answer.

"I dare say you are clever, though," continued Bessie, by way of solace. "What can you do? Can you play on the piano?"

"A little – and that is one of my paintings over the chimney-piece."

"Well, that is beautiful, Miss Jane! And have you learnt French?"

"Yes, Bessie; I can both read it and speak it."

"Oh, you are quite a lady, Miss Jane! There was something I wanted to ask you. Have you ever heard anything from your father's kinsfolk, the Eyres?"

"Never in my life."

"Well, one day, nearly seven years ago, a Mr Eyre came to Gateshead and wanted to see you; Missis said you were at school fifty miles off. He seemed so much disappointed, for he was going on a voyage to a foreign country in a day or two. He looked quite a gentleman, and I believe he was your father's brother."

"What foreign country was he going to, Bessie?"

## Chapter 10

"Madeira," she said. "He did not stay many minutes in the house."

Bessie and I conversed about old times an hour longer, and then she was obliged to leave me.

The next morning at Lowton I mounted the vehicle which was to bear me to new duties and a new life in the unknown environs of Millcote.

# Chapter 11

A new chapter in a novel is like a new scene in a play, and when I draw up the curtain this time, reader, you must imagine a room in the George Inn at Millcote, by an excellent fire, near which I sit in my cloak and bonnet; my muff and umbrella lie on the table, and I am warming away the numbness and chill contracted by sixteen hours journey, having left Lowton at four o'clock a.m., and the Millcote town clock is now just striking eight.

"Is your name Eyre, Miss?" asked a waiter.

"Yes."

"Person here waiting for you."

I jumped up, took my possessions, and hastened outside. A man stood by the open door and in the lamp-lit street I dimly saw a small carriage. He hoisted my luggage on to the vehicle, fastened the door, climbed to his own seat outside and we set off. I leaned back in the comfortable conveyance and shortly let down the window to look out: Millcote was far behind us.

The roads were heavy, the night misty; my conductor let his horse walk all the way, meaning that it was two hours before we reached Thornfield. We passed a church; I saw its low broad tower against the sky and its bell was tolling a quarter; I saw a narrow galaxy of lights too, on a hillside, marking a village or hamlet. About ten minutes after, the driver got down and opened a pair of gates: we passed through, and they clashed to behind us. We now slowly ascended a drive and came upon the long front of a house; candlelight gleamed from one curtained bow-window; all the rest were dark. The carriage stopped at the front door; it was opened by a maid-servant; I alighted and went in.

## Chapter 11

"Will you walk this way, ma'am?" said the girl, and I followed her across a square hall with high doors all round. She ushered me into a snug small room with a round table by a cheerful fire and an arm-chair high-backed and old-fashioned, wherein sat the neatest imaginable little elderly lady, in widow's cap, black silk gown, and snowy muslin apron; exactly like what I had fancied Mrs Fairfax, only less stately and milder looking. She was occupied in knitting; a large cat sat demurely at her feet. A more reassuring introduction for a new governess could scarcely be conceived. There was no grandeur to overwhelm, no stateliness to embarrass, and then, as I entered, the old lady got up and promptly and kindly came forward to meet me.

"How do you do, my dear? I am afraid you have had a tedious ride. You must be cold; come to the fire."

"Mrs Fairfax, I suppose?" said I.

"Yes, you are right: do sit down. Now, then, draw nearer to the fire. I will ask Leah for some sandwiches and see your luggage is carried into your room," she said and bustled out.

I felt rather confused at being the object of more attention than I had ever before received, and that, too, shown by my employer and superior.

"Shall I have the pleasure of seeing Miss Fairfax to-night?" I asked, when I had partaken of what she offered me.

"Miss Fairfax? Oh, you mean Miss Varens! Varens is the name of your future pupil."

"Indeed! Then she is not your daughter?"

"No – I have no family." she replied. "I am so glad you are come; it will be quite pleasant living here now with a companion, for Thornfield is a fine old hall, rather neglected of late years perhaps, but still it is a respectable place. Yet you know in winter-time one feels dreary and quite alone in the best quarters."

My heart really warmed to the worthy lady as I heard her talk, and I drew my chair a little nearer to her and expressed my sincere wish that she might find my company as agreeable as she anticipated.

"But I'll not keep you sitting up late to-night," said she. "It is twelve now and you have been travelling all day: you must feel tired. If you have got your feet well warmed, I'll show you your bedroom."

She took her candle and led the way upstairs. The steps and banisters were of oak; the staircase window was high and latticed; both it and the long gallery into which the bedroom doors opened looked as if they belonged to a church rather than a house. A very chill and vault-like air pervaded the stairs and gallery, suggesting cheerless ideas of space and solitude, and I was glad, when finally ushered into my chamber, to find it of small dimensions, and furnished in ordinary, modern style.

When Mrs Fairfax had bidden me a kind good-night and I had fastened my door, I gazed leisurely round, realising that, after a day of bodily fatigue and mental anxiety, I was now at last in a safe haven. At once weary and content, I slept soon and soundly.

When I awoke it was broad day. I dressed myself with care, obliged to be plain – for I had no article of attire that was not made with extreme simplicity – I was still by nature solicitous to be neat. It was not my habit to be disregardful of appearance; on the contrary, I ever wished to look as well as I could, and as my want of beauty would permit. I sometimes regretted that I was not handsomer; I sometimes wished to have rosy cheeks, a straight nose and small cherry mouth; I desired to be tall, stately, and finely developed in figure; I felt it a misfortune that I was so little, so pale, and had features so irregular and so marked. However, when I had brushed my hair very smooth and put on my black frock and adjusted my clean white collar, I thought I should do respectably enough to appear before Mrs Fairfax and my new pupil. Having opened my chamber window and left all things straight and neat, I ventured forth.

Downstairs, the hall-door stood open; it was a fine autumn morning. I was enjoying the calm prospect and pleasant fresh air when Mrs Fairfax appeared at the door.

"What! Out already? How do you like Thornfield?" she asked. I told her I liked it very much.

"Yes," she said, "it is a pretty place, but I fear it will be getting out of order, unless Mr Rochester should take it into his head to come and reside here

## Chapter 11

permanently; great houses and fine grounds require the presence of the proprietor."

"Mr Rochester!" I exclaimed. "Who is he?"

"The owner of Thornfield," she responded quietly. "Did you not know he was called Rochester?"

Of course I did not – I had never heard of him before, but the old lady seemed to regard his existence as a universally understood fact, with which everybody must be acquainted by instinct.

"I thought," I continued, "Thornfield belonged to you."

"To me? Bless you, child; what an idea! To me! I am only the housekeeper – the manager."

"And the little girl – my pupil!"

"She is Mr Rochester's ward. Here she comes, with her nurse, Sophie."

I looked at my pupil, who did not at first appear to notice me. She was perhaps seven or eight years old, slightly built, with a pale, small-featured face and hair falling in curls to her waist.

"Good morning, Miss Adèle," said Mrs Fairfax. "Come and speak to the lady who is to teach you and to make you a clever woman some day." She approached.

"C'est là ma gouvernante!" said she, pointing to me.

I was amazed at hearing the French language. Fortunately, I had had the advantage of being taught French by a French lady, and having made efforts to apply myself daily, I had acquired a certain degree of proficiency in the language, meaning Adèle could chatter to me fluently and I understood her very well.

I discovered she had lived with her mother until she died. She told me her mama used to teach her to dance and sing, and that a great many gentlemen and ladies came to see her mama. She offered to sing for me, choosing a song from some opera. It was about a forsaken lady, who desires her attendant to adorn her in her brightest jewels and richest robes in order to meet her false lover at a ball. The subject seemed strangely chosen for an infant singer.

Adèle also explained how when her mother died, Mr Rochester asked her if she would like to go and live with him in England. She had met Mr Rochester before, and he was always kind to her and gave her pretty dresses and toys, so she had agreed.

After breakfast, Adèle and I withdrew to the library, which was to be used as the schoolroom. I found my pupil disinclined to apply herself; she had not been used to regular occupation of any kind. I talked to her a great deal and got her to learn a little, so that when the morning had advanced to noon, I allowed her to return to her nurse.

As I was going upstairs to my room, Mrs Fairfax called to me from the dining-room nearby.

"In what good order you keep these rooms, Mrs Fairfax!" said I. "One would think they were inhabited daily."

"Why, Miss Eyre, though Mr Rochester's visits here are rare, they are always sudden and unexpected, so it is best to keep the rooms in readiness."

"Is Mr Rochester generally liked?" I dared ask.

"Oh, yes, the family have always been respected here. Almost all the land in this neighbourhood, as far as you can see, has belonged to the Rochesters for longer than people can remember."

"But do you like him? Is he liked for himself? What, in short, is his character?"

"I have no cause not to like him, and I believe he is considered a fair and generous landlord by his tenants. He is rather peculiar, perhaps: he has travelled a great deal, and seen a great deal of the world. I dare say he is clever, but I never had much conversation with him."

"In what way is he peculiar?"

"I don't know – it is not easy to describe – nothing striking, but you feel it when he speaks to you; you cannot be always sure whether he is in jest or earnest. But he is a very good master."

## Chapter 11

This was all the account I got from Mrs Fairfax of her employer and mine; she would not be drawn. Mr Rochester was Mr Rochester in her eyes; a gentleman, a landed proprietor – nothing more.

When we left the dining-room, she showed me over the rest of the house and I followed her upstairs and downstairs, admiring as I went, for all was well arranged and handsome.

At last, we reached the third storey of Thornfield Hall where the rooms, though dark and low, were interesting from their air of antiquity. They contained furniture removed here from the rooms below, some of which must have been a hundred years old. All these relics gave to the aspect of a home of the past: a shrine of memory.

"Do the servants sleep in these rooms?" I asked.

"No, no one ever sleeps here: one would almost say that, if there were a ghost at Thornfield Hall, this would be its haunt."

"So, I think you have no ghost, then?"

"None that I ever heard of," returned Mrs Fairfax, smiling and moving away.

I lingered in the long passage which was narrow, low, and dim, with only one little window at the far end, and looking, with its two rows of small black doors all shut, like a corridor in some Bluebeard's castle.

While I paced softly on, the last sound I expected to hear in so still a region, a laugh, struck my ear. It was a curious laugh: distinct, formal, mirthless. I stopped. The sound ceased, only for an instant; it began again, louder.

"Mrs Fairfax!" I called out, for she was already descending the great stairs. "Did you hear that loud laugh? Who is it?"

"Some of the servants, very likely," she answered. "Perhaps Grace Poole. I often hear her; she sews in one of these rooms. Sometimes Leah is with her; they are frequently noisy together."

The laugh came again and ended in an odd murmur.

"Grace!" exclaimed Mrs Fairfax.

I really did not expect any Grace to answer, but the door nearest me opened and a servant came out – a woman of between thirty and forty with a hard, plain face and the last person one might consider to be a ghost.

"Too much noise, Grace," said Mrs Fairfax. "Remember directions!" Grace curtseyed silently and went in.

We continued our return to the light and cheerful region below and found dinner ready and waiting for us in Mrs Fairfax's room.

# Chapter 12

Mrs Fairfax turned out to be a kind-natured woman, of competent education and average intelligence. My pupil was a lively child, who had been spoilt and indulged, but as she was committed entirely to my care, she soon became obedient and teachable. She had no great talents, but she made reasonable progress, and by her efforts to please inspired me, in return, with a degree of attachment.

Now and then, when I took a walk by myself in the grounds; when I went down to the gates and looked through them along the road; or when I climbed the three staircases, raised the trap-door of the attic, and looked out afar over field and hill, and along dim sky-line – then I longed for a power of vision which might overpass that limit; which might reach the busy world, towns, regions full of life I had heard of but never seen. Then I desired more experience than I possessed, more of intercourse with my kind, of acquaintance with variety of character, than was here within my reach. I valued what was good in Mrs Fairfax, and what was good in Adèle, but I believed in the existence of other and more vivid kinds of goodness. Who blames me? Many, no doubt, and I shall be called discontented. I could not help it: the restlessness was in my nature; it agitated me to pain sometimes. Then my sole relief was to walk along the corridor of the third storey, backwards and forwards, and allow my mind's eye to dwell on whatever bright visions rose before it and, best of all, to open my inward ear to a tale my imagination created, quickened with all of life, fire, feeling, that I desired and had not in my actual existence.

It is in vain to say human beings ought to be satisfied with tranquillity: they must have action, and they will make it if they cannot find it. Millions are condemned to a stiller doom than mine, and millions are in silent revolt against their lot. Women are supposed to be very calm generally, but women feel just as men feel; they suffer from too rigid a restraint, too absolute a stagnation, precisely as men would suffer, and it is narrow-minded in their more privileged fellow-creatures to say that they ought to confine themselves to making puddings and knitting stockings, to playing on the piano and embroidering bags.

When thus alone, I not unfrequently heard Grace Poole's laugh: the same peal, the same low, slow ha! ha! which, when first heard, had thrilled me. I heard, too, her eccentric murmurs, stranger than her laugh. There were days when she was quite silent, but there were others when I could not account for the sounds she made. Sometimes I saw her: she would come out of her room with a basin, or a plate, or a tray in her hand, go down to the kitchen and shortly return. I made some attempts to draw her into conversation, but she seemed a person of few words.

One afternoon in January, Mrs Fairfax had begged a holiday for Adèle because she had a cold. It was a fine, calm day, though very cold. Mrs Fairfax had just written a letter which was waiting to be posted, so I put on my bonnet and cloak and volunteered to carry it to Hay; the distance, two miles, would be a pleasant winter afternoon walk.

The ground was hard; the air was still; my road was lonely. I was a mile from Thornfield, in a lane noted for wild roses in summer and even now possessing a few coral treasures in hips and haws. Having reached the middle of the lane, I sat down on a stile. On the hill-top above me sat the rising moon, pale yet as a cloud but brightening momentarily.

A rude noise broke: a horse was coming. It was very near but not yet in sight, when I heard a rush under the hedge and, close by the hazel stems, glided a great dog, whose black and white colour made him a distinct object against the trees. The horse followed – a tall steed, and on its back a rider. It was only a traveller taking the short cut to Millcote. He passed, and I went on; a few steps, and I turned: a sliding sound, an exclamation and a clattering tumble, arrested my attention. Man and horse were down; they had slipped on the sheet of ice which glazed the causeway. The dog came bounding back and seeing his master in a predicament, and hearing the horse groan, barked till the evening hills echoed the sound. He snuffed round the prostrate group, and then he ran up to me; it was all he could do – there was no other help at hand to summon. I obeyed him, and walked down to the traveller, by this time struggling himself free of his steed. His efforts were so vigorous I thought he could not be much hurt, but I asked him the question –

"Are you injured, sir?"

I think he was swearing, which prevented him from replying to me directly.

"Can I do anything?" I asked again.

"You must just stand on one side," he answered as he rose, first to his knees and then to his feet. I did, whereupon began a heaving, stamping, clattering process, accompanied by a barking and baying. This was finally fortunate: the horse was re-established and the dog was silenced with a "Down, Pilot!" The traveller now, stooping, felt his foot and leg as if trying whether they were sound; apparently something ailed them, for he halted and sat down.

I now drew near him again.

"If you are hurt and want help, sir, I can fetch someone either from Thornfield Hall or from Hay."

"Thank you, I shall do; I have no broken bones – only a sprain." Again, he stood up and tried his foot, but the result extorted an involuntary "Ugh!"

Something of daylight still lingered, and the moon was waxing bright: I could see him plainly. His figure was enveloped in a riding cloak, fur collared and steel clasped; its details were not apparent, but I traced the general points of middle height and considerable breadth of chest. He had a dark face, with stern features and a heavy brow; his eyes and gathered eyebrows looked ireful and thwarted just now; he was past youth but had not reached middle-age – perhaps he might be thirty-five. I felt no fear of him and but little shyness. Had he been a handsome, heroic-looking young gentleman, I should not have dared to stand thus questioning him against his will and offering my services unasked. I had hardly ever seen a handsome youth, never in my life spoken to one.

If even this stranger had smiled and been good-humoured to me when I addressed him, I should have gone on my way and not felt any vocation to renew inquiries, but the frown, the roughness of the traveller, set me at my ease. I retained my station when he waved to me to go, and announced –

"I cannot think of leaving you, sir, at so late an hour, in this solitary lane, till I see you are fit to mount your horse."

He looked at me when I said this; he had hardly turned his eyes in my direction before.

"I should think you ought to be at home yourself," said he, "if you have a home in this neighbourhood. Where do you come from?"

"From just below, and I am not at all afraid of being out late when it is moonlight. I will run over to Hay for you with pleasure, if you wish it; indeed, I am going there to post a letter."

"You live just below – do you mean at that house with the battlements?" pointing to Thornfield Hall.

"Yes, sir."

"Whose house is it?"

"Mr Rochester's."

"Do you know Mr Rochester?"

"No, I have never seen him."

"He is not resident, then?"

"No."

"Can you tell me where he is?"

"I cannot."

"You are not a servant at the hall, of course. You are—" He stopped, ran his eye over my dress, which, as usual, was quite simple, not half fine enough for a lady's-maid. He seemed puzzled to decide what I was; I helped him.

"I am the governess."

# Chapter 12

"Ah, the governess!" he repeated. "Deuce take me, if I had not forgotten! The governess!" In two minutes he rose from the stile; his face expressed pain when he tried to move.

"I cannot commission you to fetch help," he said, "but you may help me a little yourself, if you will be so kind."

"Yes, sir."

"You have not an umbrella that I can use as a stick?"

"No."

"Excuse me," he continued, "necessity compels me to make you useful." He laid a heavy hand on my shoulder, and leaning on me with some stress, limped to his horse. Having once caught the bridle, he mastered it directly and sprang to his saddle, grimacing grimly as he made the effort, for it wrenched his sprain.

"Now," said he, releasing his under lip from a hard bite, "just hand me my whip; it lies there under the hedge."

I sought it and found it.

"Thank you. Now make haste with the letter to Hay and return as fast as you can."

A touch of a spurred heel made his horse first start and rear, and then bound away; the dog rushed in his traces; all three vanished,

I took up my muff and walked on. The incident had occurred and was gone for me. It *was* an incident of no moment, no romance, no interest in a sense, yet it marked with change one single hour of a monotonous life. The new face, too, was like a new picture introduced to the gallery of memory, and it was dissimilar to all the others hanging there; firstly, because it was masculine and, secondly, because it was dark, strong, and stern. When I came to the stile, I stopped a minute, looked round and listened, with an idea that a horse's hoofs might ring on the causeway again, and that a rider in a cloak might be again apparent. I heard only the faintest waft of wind roaming fitful among the trees round Thornfield, and when I glanced down in the direction of the murmur, my eye caught a light kindling in a window; it reminded me that I was late and I hurried on.

I did not like re-entering Thornfield. To pass its threshold was to return to stagnation; to cross the silent hall and then to meet tranquil Mrs Fairfax and spend the long winter evening with her, and her only, was to quell wholly the faint excitement wakened by my walk.

I lingered at the gates; I lingered on the lawn; I paced backwards and forwards on the pavement. Both my eyes and spirit seemed drawn from the gloomy house to that sky expanded before me. Little things recall us to earth: the clock struck in the hall and that sufficed. I turned from moon and stars, opened a side-door, and went in.

I hastened to Mrs Fairfax's room; there was a fire there but no candle and no Mrs Fairfax. Instead, all alone, sitting upright on the rug, I beheld a great black and white long-haired dog, just like the dog of the lane. It was so like it that I went forward and said, "Pilot," and the thing got up and came to me and snuffed me. I rang the bell, for I wanted a candle; Leah entered.

"What dog is this?"

"He came with master."

"With whom?"

"With master – Mr Rochester – he is just arrived."

"Indeed! And is Mrs Fairfax with him?"

"Yes, and Miss Adèle; they are in the dining-room and John is gone for a surgeon, for master has had an accident. His horse fell and his ankle is sprained."

"Did the horse fall in Hay Lane?"

"Yes, coming down-hill – it slipped on some ice."

# Chapter 13

Mr Rochester went to bed early that night, nor did he rise soon next morning. When he did come down, his agent and some of his tenants were arrived, waiting to speak with him.

Adèle and I had now to vacate the library: it would be used as a reception-room for callers. A fire was lit in an apartment upstairs and there I carried our books for the future schoolroom. Thornfield Hall was a changed place: no longer silent as a church, it echoed every hour or two to a knock at the door, or a clang of the bell and new voices spoke in different keys below; I liked it better.

Adèle was not easy to teach that day; she kept running to the door and looking over the banisters to get a glimpse of Mr Rochester. When I got a little angry and made her sit still, she continued to talk incessantly of her "ami, Monsieur Edouard Fairfax de Rochester", and to conjecture what presents he had brought her.

The afternoon was wild and snowy, and we passed it in the schoolroom. At dark I allowed Adèle to put away books and work and to run downstairs, for, from the comparative silence below, and from the cessation of appeals to the doorbell, I conjectured that Mr Rochester was now at liberty.

Left alone, I let down the curtain and went back to the fireside when Mrs Fairfax came in, scattering some heavy, unwelcome thoughts that were beginning to throng on my solitude.

"Mr Rochester would be glad if you and your pupil would take tea with him in the drawing-room this evening," said she.

We went downstairs into the dining-room and, passing the arch, whose curtain was now dropped, entered the elegant recess beyond.

Two wax candles stood lighted on the table, and two on the mantelpiece; basking in the light and heat of a superb fire, lay Pilot – Adèle knelt near him. Half reclined on a couch appeared Mr Rochester, his foot supported by the cushion. The fire shone full on his face. I knew my traveller with his square forehead, made squarer by the horizontal sweep of his black hair. I recognised his decisive nose, more remarkable for character than beauty; his full nostrils; his grim mouth, chin, and jaw. His shape, now divested of cloak, was a good figure in the athletic sense of the term – broad chested and thin flanked, though neither tall nor graceful.

Mr Rochester must have been aware of the entrance of Mrs Fairfax and myself, but he never lifted his head as we approached.

"Here is Miss Eyre, sir," said Mrs Fairfax, in her quiet way. He bowed, not taking his eyes from the group of the dog and child.

"Let Miss Eyre be seated," said he.

He went on as a statue would; he neither spoke nor moved. Mrs Fairfax seemed to think it necessary that someone should be amiable and she began to talk. Kindly, as usual, she condoled with him on the pressure of business he had had all day, on the annoyance it must have been to him with that painful sprain, then she commended his patience and perseverance.

"Madam, I should like some tea," was the sole rejoinder she got, and when the tray came, I and Adèle went to the table but the master did not leave his couch.

"Will you hand Mr Rochester's cup?" said Mrs Fairfax to me. "Adèle might perhaps spill it."

As he took the cup from my hand, Adèle, thinking the moment propitious for making a request in my favour, cried out –

"N'est-ce pas, monsieur, qu'il y a un cadeau pour Mademoiselle Eyre dans votre petit coffre?"

"Who talks of cadeaux?" said he gruffly. "Did you expect a present, Miss Eyre? Are you fond of presents?" and he searched my face with eyes that I saw were dark, irate, and piercing.

## Chapter 13

"I have little experience of them; they are generally thought pleasant things."

"Generally thought? But what do you think?"

"I should be obliged to take time, sir, before I could give you an answer."

"Miss Eyre, you are not so unsophisticated as Adèle: she demands a 'cadeau,' clamorously, the moment she sees me; you beat about the bush."

"Because I have less confidence in my rewards than Adèle has and have done nothing to entitle me to such an acknowledgment."

"Oh, don't fall back on over-modesty! I have examined Adèle and find you have taken great pains with her: she is not bright, she has no talents, yet in a short time she has made much improvement."

"Sir, you have now given me my 'cadeau'; I am obliged to you: it is what teachers most covet – praise of their pupils' progress."

"Come to the fire," said the master, when the tray was taken away. "You have been resident in my house three months?"

"Yes, sir."

"And you came from—?"

"From Lowood school."

"Ah! A charitable concern. How long were you there?"

"Eight years."

"Eight years! You must be tenacious of life. No wonder you have rather the look of another world. When you came on me in Hay Lane last night, I thought unaccountably of fairy tales, and had half a mind to demand whether you had bewitched my horse. Who are your parents?"

"I have none."

"I thought not. You must have some sort of kinsfolk: uncles and aunts?"

"No, none that I ever saw."

"And your home?"

"I have none."

"Who recommended you to come here?"

"I advertised and Mrs Fairfax answered my advertisement."

"Yes," said the good lady, "and I am daily thankful for the choice Providence led me to make. Miss Eyre has been an invaluable companion to me, and a kind and careful teacher to Adèle."

"Don't trouble yourself to give her a character," returned Mr Rochester, "praise will not bias me. She began by felling my horse. I have to thank her for this sprain."

The widow looked bewildered.

"What age were you when you went to Lowood?"

"About ten."

"And you stayed there eight years; you are now, then, eighteen? And now what did you learn at Lowood? Can you play?"

"A little."

"Of course, that is the established answer. Go into the library; take a candle with you; leave the door open; sit down to the piano and play a tune."

I departed, obeying his directions.

"Enough!" he called out in a few minutes. "You play a little, I see, like any other English schoolgirl; perhaps rather better than some, but not well."

I closed the piano and returned. Mr Rochester continued –

"Adèle showed me some sketches this morning. Fetch me your portfolio."

I brought the portfolio from the library.

He deliberately scrutinised each sketch and painting. Two he laid aside.

"I perceive those pictures were done by one hand; was that hand yours?"

"Yes."

## Chapter 13

"And when did you find time to do them? They have taken much time, and some thought."

"I did them in the last two vacations I spent at Lowood."

"Where did you get your copies?"

"Out of my head."

He spread the pictures before him and surveyed them alternately.

While he is so occupied, I will tell you, reader, what they are and first, I must premise that they are nothing wonderful.

The first represented clouds, low and livid, rolling over a swollen sea. One gleam of light lifted into relief a half-submerged mast, on which sat a cormorant, dark and large; its beak held a gold bracelet. Sinking below the bird and mast, a drowned corpse glanced through the green water; a fair arm was the only limb clearly visible, whence the bracelet had been washed or torn.

The second picture showed the pinnacle of an iceberg piercing a polar winter sky; in the foreground rose a colossal head, resting against the iceberg. Two thin hands drew up a veil – a brow white as bone, and an eye, hollow and fixed, blank of meaning but for the glassiness of despair, alone were visible. Above the temples gleamed a pale crescent: "the likeness of a kingly crown."

"Were you happy when you painted these pictures?" asked Mr Rochester presently.

"I was absorbed, sir, yes, and I was happy. To paint them, in short, was to enjoy one of the keenest pleasures I have ever known."

"The drawings are, for a school-girl, peculiar. As to the thoughts, they are elfish. And what meaning is that in their solemn depth? And who taught you to paint wind? There! Put the drawings away!"

Then looking at his watch, he said abruptly, "It is nine o'clock: what are you about, Miss Eyre, to let Adèle sit up so long? Take her to bed."

"I wish you all good-night," said he, making a movement of the hand towards the door, in token that he was tired of our company, and wished to dismiss us. Mrs Fairfax folded up her knitting; I took my portfolio; we curtseyed to him, received a frigid bow in return, and so withdrew.

"You said Mr Rochester was not strikingly peculiar, Mrs Fairfax," I observed, when I rejoined her in her room, after putting Adèle to bed.

"Well, is he?"

"I think so: he is very changeful and abrupt."

"True: no doubt he may appear so to a stranger, but I am so accustomed to his manner, I never think of it, and then, if he has peculiarities of temper, allowance should be made."

"Why?"

"Family troubles, for one thing."

"But he has no family."

"Not now, but he has had – or, at least, relatives. He lost his elder brother a few years since."

"His elder brother?"

"Yes. The present Mr Rochester has not been very long in possession of the property, only about nine years."

"Nine years is a tolerable time. Was he so very fond of his brother?"

"Why, no. I believe there were some misunderstandings between them. Mr Rowland Rochester prejudiced his father against Mr Edward. Old Mr Rochester was fond of money and, anxious that Mr Edward should have wealth, took steps that were not quite fair, making a great deal of mischief. The old gentleman and Mr Rowland combined to bring Mr Edward into a painful position, for the sake of making his fortune. What the precise nature of that position was I never clearly knew, but his spirit could not accept what he had to suffer. He broke with his family and has led an unsettled kind of life. I don't think he has ever been resident at Thornfield for a fortnight together. Indeed, he shuns the old place."

"Why should he shun it?"

"Perhaps he thinks it gloomy."

## Chapter 13

The answer was evasive, but Mrs Fairfax either could not, or would not, give me more information of the origin and nature of Mr Rochester's trials. She claimed they were a mystery to herself. It was evident, indeed, that she wished me to drop the subject, which I did accordingly.

# Chapter 14

For several days I saw little of Mr Rochester. In the mornings he seemed much engaged with business, and, in the afternoon, gentlemen from Millcote or the neighbourhood called, and sometimes stayed to dine with him.

But one night a message came that I and Adèle were to go downstairs. I brushed Adèle's hair and made her neat.

Mr Rochester, in his damask-covered chair, looked different, not quite so stern – much less gloomy. There was a smile on his lips and his eyes sparkled, whether with wine or not, I am not sure, but I think it very probable.

"Miss Eyre, draw your chair a little farther forward: you are too far back; I cannot see you without disturbing my position in this comfortable chair, which I have no mind to do."

I did as I was bid. He had been looking two minutes at the fire and I had been looking the same length of time at him, when, turning suddenly, he caught my gaze.

"You examine me, Miss Eyre," said he. "Do you think me handsome?"

The answer somehow slipped from my tongue before I was aware. "No, sir."

"Ah! By my word! There is something singular about you," said he. "You are obliged to grant a reply, which, if not blunt, is at least brusque."

"Sir, I was too plain; I beg your pardon. I ought to have replied that tastes mostly differ and that beauty is of little consequence, or something of that sort."

# Chapter 14

"You ought to have replied no such thing. Beauty of little consequence, indeed! Go on: what fault do you find with me?"

"Mr Rochester, allow me to disown my first answer. It was only a blunder."

"Just so, and you shall be answerable for it. Criticise me: does my forehead not please you?"

He lifted up the sable waves of hair which lay over his brow and showed a solid enough mass of intellectual organs.

"Far from it, sir. You would, perhaps, think me rude if I inquired in return whether you are a philanthropist?"

"No, young lady, I am not a general philanthropist, but I bear a conscience. When I was as old as you, I was a feeling fellow enough, but Fortune has knocked me about since; she has even kneaded me with her knuckles, and now I am hard and tough as an India-rubber ball. Pervious, though, through a chink or two still, and with one sentient point in the middle of the lump. Does that leave hope for me?"

"Hope of what, sir?"

"Of my re-transformation from India-rubber back to flesh?"

"Decidedly he has had too much wine," I thought, and I did not know what answer to make. How could I tell whether he was capable of being re-transformed?

"You look puzzled, Miss Eyre, and though you are not pretty any more than I am handsome, a puzzled air becomes you."

He rose from his chair and stood, leaning his arm on the marble mantlepiece.

"I am disposed to be gregarious and communicative to-night," he said, "and that is why I sent for you; the fire and the chandelier were not sufficient company for me, nor would Pilot have been, for none of these can talk. It would please me now to learn more of you – therefore speak."

Instead of speaking, I smiled, and not a submissive smile either.

"Speak," he urged.

"What about, sir?"

"Whatever you like."

Accordingly, I sat and said nothing. "If he expects me to talk for the mere sake of talking, he will find he has addressed himself to the wrong person," I thought.

"You are dumb, Miss Eyre."

He bent his head a little towards me and with a single hasty glance seemed to dive into my eyes.

"Stubborn?" he said, "and annoyed. I don't wish to treat you like an inferior; I claim only such superiority as must result from twenty years' difference in age, and it is by virtue of this superiority, and this alone, that I desire you to have the goodness to talk to me a little now and divert my thoughts."

"I am willing to amuse you, if I can, sir, but I cannot introduce a topic, because how do I know what will interest you? Ask me questions and I will do my best to answer them."

"Then, in the first place, do you agree with me that I have a right to be a little masterful because I am old enough to be your father, and have battled through a varied experience with many men of many nations, and roamed over half the globe, while you have lived quietly with one set of people in one house?"

"Do as you please, sir."

"That is no answer, or rather, it is a very irritating, because a very evasive one. Reply clearly."

"I don't think, sir, you have a right to command me merely because you are older than I, or because you have seen more of the world than I have; your claim to superiority depends on the use you have made of your time and experience."

"Leaving superiority out of the question, then, you must still agree to receive my orders now and then, without being piqued or hurt by the tone of command. Will you?"

## Chapter 14

I smiled; I thought to myself, "Mr Rochester is peculiar – he seems to forget that he pays me £30 per annum for receiving his orders."

"The smile is very well," said he, catching instantly the passing expression, "but speak too."

"I was thinking, sir, that very few masters would trouble themselves to inquire whether or not their paid subordinates were hurt by their orders."

"Paid subordinates! What! You are my paid subordinate, are you? Oh yes, I had forgotten the salary! Well then, on that ground, will you agree to let me hector a little?"

"No, sir, not on that ground, but, on the ground that you did forget it, and that you care whether or not a dependent is comfortable in his dependency, I agree heartily."

"I have plenty of faults: I know it, and I don't wish to excuse them. I started, or rather was thrust on to a wrong tack, at the age of one-and-twenty and have never recovered the right course since, but I might have been very different; I might have been as good as you – wiser – almost as stainless. I envy you your peace of mind, your clean conscience, your unpolluted memory."

"How was your memory when you were eighteen, sir?"

"All right then. I was your equal at eighteen – quite your equal. Nature meant me to be, on the whole, a good man, Miss Eyre; one of the better kind, and you see I am not so. Take my word for it – I am not a villain; you are not to attribute to me any such bad eminence. Do you wonder that I reveal this to you? Know that in your future life you will often find yourself the involuntary confidant of your acquaintances' secrets: people will instinctively find out, as I have done, that it is not your forte to tell of yourself, but to listen while others talk of themselves with a kind of innate sympathy. Therefore, I proceed almost as freely as if I were writing my thoughts in a diary. When fate wronged me, I had not the wisdom to remain cool: I turned desperate, then I degenerated. Dread remorse when you are tempted to err, Miss Eyre; remorse is the poison of life."

"Repentance is said to be its cure, sir."

"It is not its cure. Reformation may be its cure, and I could reform – I have strength yet for that – but where is the use of thinking of it, hampered, burdened, cursed as I am? Besides, since happiness is irrevocably denied me, I have a right to get pleasure out of life, and I will get it, cost what it may. You have no right to preach to me, as you have not passed the porch of life and are absolutely unacquainted with its mysteries."

"I only remind you of your own words, sir, but to speak truth, I cannot keep up the conversation, because it has got out of my depth. Only one thing, I know: you said you were not as good as you should like to be and that you regretted your own imperfection. It seems to me that if you tried hard, you would in time find it possible to become what you yourself would approve, and that if from this day you began with resolution to correct your thoughts and actions, you would in a few years have laid up a new and stainless store of recollections, to which you might revert with pleasure."

"Justly thought; rightly said, Miss Eyre, and at this moment I am laying down good intentions, which I believe durable as flint. My associates and pursuits shall be other than they have been."

"May they be right then," I said, as I rose, deeming it useless to continue a discourse which was all darkness to me.

"Where are you going?"

"To put Adèle to bed: it is past her bedtime."

"You are afraid of me because I talk like a Sphynx."

"Your language is enigmatical, sir, but I am certainly not afraid."

"Do you never laugh, Miss Eyre? Don't trouble yourself to answer – I see you laugh rarely, but you can laugh very merrily. The Lowood constraint still clings to you, controlling your features, muffling your voice, and restricting your limbs. You fear in the presence of a man and a brother – or father, or master, or what you will – to smile too gaily, speak too freely, or move too quickly, but, in time, I think you will learn to be natural with me, as I find it impossible to be conventional with you. I see at intervals the glance of a curious sort of bird through the close-set bars of a cage:

## Chapter 14

a vivid, restless, resolute captive is there. Were it but free, it would soar cloud-high."

"It has struck nine, sir. Good night."

"Good-night."

# Chapter 15

One afternoon, Mr Rochester chanced to meet me and Adèle in the grounds. She played with Pilot, while he asked me to walk up and down a long beech avenue.

He said that she was the daughter of a French opera-dancer, Céline Varens, towards whom he had once cherished a "grande passion." This passion Céline had professed to return with even superior ardour.

"And, Miss Eyre, so much was I flattered by this that I installed her in an hotel, and gave her servants, a carriage, cashmeres and diamonds, like any other romantic fool. Happening to call one evening, I found Céline out, but it was a warm night, so I opened the window to step out on to the balcony. It was moonlight and very still and serene. I sat down and took out a cigar.

"Watching the carriages that rolled along the fashionable streets towards the neighbouring opera-house, I recognised the 'voiture' I had given Céline. She was returning; my heart thumped with impatience. The carriage stopped; I knew her instantly as she skipped from the carriage-step. Bending over the balcony, I was about to murmur 'Mon ange', when a figure jumped from the carriage after her.

"You never felt jealousy, did you, Miss Eyre? Of course not, because you never felt love. But – mark my words – you will come some day to a craggy pass in the channel, where the whole of life's stream will be broken up into whirl and tumult, foam and noise; either you will be dashed to atoms on crag points, or lifted up and borne on by some master-wave into a calmer current – as I am now."

He paused; Thornfield Hall was before us. Lifting his eye to its battlements, he cast over them a glare such as I never saw before or since.

## Chapter 15

Pain, shame, ire, impatience, disgust, detestation, seemed momentarily to hold a quivering conflict in the large pupil dilating under his ebon eyebrow, but another feeling rose and triumphed: he went on –

"When I saw my charmer thus come in accompanied by a cavalier, the green snake of jealousy, rising on undulating coils, ate its way into my heart's core. I remained in the balcony from which I could take observations. The couple both removed their cloaks and there was 'the Varens,' shining in satin and jewels – my gifts of course – and there was her companion, and I knew him for a brainless and vicious youth whom I had sometimes met.

"A card of mine lay on the table; this being perceived, brought my name under discussion. They insulted me as coarsely as they could, especially Céline, who waxed on my personal defects – deformities, she termed them.

"I walked in upon them; liberated Céline from my protection; gave her notice to vacate her hotel; disregarded screams, hysterics, prayers, protestations, convulsions, and made an appointment with the vicomte for a meeting at the Bois de Boulogne. Next morning, I left a bullet in one of his poor etiolated arms and thought I had done with the whole crew. But unluckily the Varens, six months before, had given me this filette Adèle, who, she affirmed, was my daughter, though I see no proofs – Pilot is more like me than she. Some years after I had broken with the mother, she abandoned her child and ran away to Italy with a musician. I acknowledged no natural claim on Adèle's part, for I am not her father, but hearing that she was quite destitute, I took the poor thing. Now you know that it is the illegitimate offspring of a French opera-girl, you will perhaps think differently of your post and protégée – Eh?"

"No: Adèle is not answerable for either her mother's faults or yours, and now that I know she is, in a sense, parentless – forsaken by her mother and disowned by you, sir – I shall cling closer to her than before."

"Well, I must go in now, and you too: it darkens."

But I stayed out a few minutes longer with Adèle and Pilot. When we went in and I had removed her bonnet and coat, I took her on my knee and kept her there an hour, allowing her to prattle as she liked. I sought in her countenance and features a likeness to Mr Rochester but found none.

After I had withdrawn to my own chamber for the night, I steadily reviewed the tale Mr Rochester had told me. The confidence he had thought fit to repose in me seemed a tribute to my discretion; I regarded and accepted it as such. His behaviour had now for some weeks been more uniform towards me than at the first. When he met me unexpectedly, he had always a word and sometimes a smile for me; when summoned, I was honoured by a cordiality of reception that made me feel I really possessed the power to amuse him. I had a keen delight in receiving the new ideas he offered, in imagining the new pictures he portrayed, and following him in thought through the new regions he disclosed.

He was imperious sometimes still, but I did not mind that; I saw it was his way. So happy, so gratified did I become with this new interest added to life, that my thin crescent-destiny seemed to enlarge; the blanks of existence were filled up; my bodily health improved; I gathered flesh and strength.

And was Mr Rochester now ugly in my eyes? No, reader: gratitude, and many associations, all pleasurable and genial, made his face the object I best liked to see; his presence in a room was more cheering than the brightest fire. Yet I had not forgotten his faults; he was moody, but I believed that his moodiness, his harshness, and his former faults had their source in some cruel cross of fate. I believed he was naturally a man of better tendencies, though for the present they hung together somewhat spoiled and tangled.

I hardly know whether I had slept or not after this musing; at any rate, I started wide awake on hearing a vague murmur, peculiar and lugubrious, which sounded, I thought, just above me. I wished I had kept my candle burning: the night was drearily dark. I rose and sat up in bed, listening. The sound was hushed.

I tried again to sleep but my heart beat anxiously: my inward tranquillity was broken. The clock, far down in the hall, struck two. Just then it seemed my chamber-door was touched, as if fingers had swept the panels in groping a way along the dark gallery outside. I said, "Who is there?" Nothing answered. I was chilled with fear.

## Chapter 15

I lay down. Silence composes the nerves, and as an unbroken hush now reigned again through the whole house, I began to feel the return of slumber. But a dream had scarcely approached my ear when it fled affrighted, scared by a marrow-freezing incident enough.

This was a demoniac laugh – low, suppressed, and deep – uttered, as it seemed, at the very keyhole of my chamber door. I thought at first the goblin-laugher stood at my bedside – or rather, crouched by my pillow – but I rose, looked round, and could see nothing; while, as I still gazed, the unnatural sound was reiterated, and I knew it came from behind the panels.

Something gurgled and moaned. Ere long, steps retreated up the gallery towards the third-storey staircase; a door had lately been made to shut in that staircase. I heard it open and close, and all was still.

"Was that Grace Poole? And is she possessed with a devil?" thought I. Impossible now to remain longer by myself; I must go to Mrs Fairfax. I hurried on my frock and a shawl; I withdrew the bolt and opened the door with a trembling hand. There was a candle burning just outside, and on the matting in the gallery. I was amazed to perceive the air quite dim, as if filled with smoke and, while looking to the right hand and left, to find whence these blue wreaths issued, I became further aware of a strong smell of burning.

Something creaked: it was a door ajar and that door was Mr Rochester's, and the smoke rushed in a cloud from thence. In an instant, I was within the chamber. Tongues of flame darted round the bed: the curtains were on fire. In the midst of blaze and vapour, Mr Rochester lay stretched motionless, in deep sleep.

"Wake! Wake!" I cried. I shook him, but he only murmured and turned: the smoke had stupefied him. Not a moment could be lost; the very sheets were kindling. I rushed to his basin and ewer, and both were filled with water. I heaved them up, deluged the bed and its occupant, flew back to my own room, brought my own water-jug, baptized the couch afresh, and, by God's aid, succeeded in extinguishing the flames which were devouring it.

"Is there a flood?" he cried.

"No, sir," I answered, "but there has been a fire. Get up, do. I will fetch you a candle."

"What have you done with me, witch, sorceress?" he demanded. "Have you plotted to drown me?"

"Somebody has plotted something; you cannot too soon find out who and what it is."

I brought the candle which still remained in the gallery. He took it from my hand, held it up, and surveyed the bed, all blackened and scorched, the sheets drenched, the carpet round swimming in water.

"What is it? And who did it?" he asked.

I briefly related to him the strange laugh I had heard in the gallery; the step ascending to the third storey; the smoke – the smell of fire which had conducted me to his room; in what state I had found matters there, and how I had deluged him with all the water I could lay hands on.

He listened very gravely; his face expressed more concern than astonishment.

"Shall I call Mrs Fairfax?" I asked.

"Not at all: just be still. You have a shawl on. If you are not warm enough, you may take my cloak yonder; wrap it about you and sit down in the arm-chair there. Now place your feet on the stool to keep them out of the wet. I shall take the candle. Remain where you are till I return. I must pay a visit to the second storey. Don't move, remember, or call anyone."

He went. I was left in total darkness. I listened for some noise but heard nothing. A very long time elapsed. I grew weary: it was cold, in spite of the cloak. Then the light once more gleamed dimly on the gallery wall, and I heard his unshod feet tread the matting.

He re-entered, pale and very gloomy. "I have found it all out," said he, setting his candle down on the washstand. "It is as I thought."

"How, sir?"

"I forget whether you said you saw anything when you opened your chamber door."

## Chapter 15

"No, sir, only the candlestick on the ground."

"But you heard an odd laugh? You have heard that laugh before, I should think, or something like it?"

"Yes, sir: there is a woman who sews here, called Grace Poole – she laughs in that way."

"Just so. Grace Poole – you have guessed it. Well, I shall reflect on the subject. Meantime, I am glad that you are the only person, besides myself, acquainted with the precise details of tonight's incident. You are to say nothing about it. I will account for this state of affairs, and now return to your own room. I shall do very well on the sofa in the library for the rest of the night."

"Good-night, then, sir," said I, departing.

He seemed surprised.

"What!" he exclaimed, "are you quitting me already, and in that way?"

"You said I might go, sir."

"But not without taking leave, not without a word or two of acknowledgment and good-will. Why, you have saved my life! Snatched me from a horrible and excruciating death! And you walk past me as if we were mutual strangers! At least shake hands."

He held out his hand; I gave him mine: he took it first in one, then in both his own.

"You have saved my life. I have a pleasure in owing you so immense a debt. I cannot say more."

He paused and gazed at me: words almost visible trembled on his lips, but his voice was checked.

"Good-night again, sir. There is no debt, benefit, burden, obligation, in the case."

"I knew," he continued, "you would do me good in some way, at some time – I saw it in your eyes when I first beheld you. My cherished preserver, good-night!"

Strange energy was in his voice, strange fire in his look.

"I am glad I happened to be awake," I said, and then I was going.

"What! You will go?"

"I am cold, sir."

"Cold? Yes, and standing in a pool! Go, then, Jane, go!" But he still retained my hand and I could not free it.

"Well, leave me," he said, relaxing his fingers, and I was gone.

I regained my couch, but never thought of sleep. Till morning dawned I was tossed on a buoyant but unquiet sea, where billows of trouble rolled under surges of joy. Too feverish to rest, I rose as soon as day dawned.

# Chapter 16

I both wished and feared to see Mr Rochester on the day which followed this sleepless night; I wanted to hear his voice again yet feared to meet his eye. During the early part of the morning, I momentarily expected his coming; I had the impression that he was sure to visit the schoolroom that day.

But the morning passed just as usual: nothing happened to interrupt the quiet course of Adèle's studies; only soon after breakfast, I heard some bustle in the neighbourhood of Mr Rochester's chamber, Mrs Fairfax's voice, and Leah's, and the cook's. There were exclamations of "What a mercy master was not burnt in his bed!" "It is always dangerous to keep a candle lit at night." "I wonder he waked nobody!"

To much discussion succeeded a sound of scrubbing and setting to rights, and when I passed the room, in going downstairs to dinner, I saw through the open door that all was again restored to complete order. Leah stood up in the window-seat, rubbing the panes of glass dimmed with smoke. I was about to address her, for I wished to know what account had been given of the affair but, on advancing, I saw a second person in the chamber – a woman sitting on a chair sewing rings to new curtains. That woman was no other than Grace Poole.

There she sat, staid and taciturn-looking, as usual. She was intent on her work; on her forehead, and in her features, was nothing of the desperation one would have expected to see marking a woman who had attempted murder. I was amazed – confounded. She looked up, while I still gazed at her. She said, "Good morning, Miss," in her usual brief manner and went on with her sewing.

"I will put her to some test," thought I.

81

"Good morning, Grace," I said. "Has anything happened here? I thought I heard the servants all talking together a while ago."

"Only master had been reading in his bed last night; he fell asleep with his candle lit, and the curtains got on fire, but, fortunately, he awoke before the bed-clothes or the wood-work caught, and contrived to quench the flames with the water in the ewer."

"A strange affair!" I said, in a low voice. Then, looking at her fixedly – "Did Mr Rochester wake nobody? Did no one hear him move?"

She again raised her eyes to me and this time she seemed to examine me warily; then she answered –

"The servants sleep so far off, you know, Miss, they would not be likely to hear. Mrs Fairfax's room and yours are the nearest to master's but Mrs Fairfax said she heard nothing." She paused, and then added in a significant tone – "You may have heard a noise, Miss?"

"I did," said I, dropping my voice, "and at first I thought it was Pilot, but I am certain I heard a laugh."

She threaded her needle with a steady hand and then observed, with perfect composure –

"It is hardly likely master would laugh, I should think, Miss, when he was in such danger. You must have been dreaming."

"I was not dreaming," I said, with some warmth. Again she looked at me.

"Have you told master that you heard a laugh?" she inquired.

"I have not had the opportunity of speaking to him this morning."

"You did not think of opening your door and looking out into the gallery?" she further asked.

She appeared to be cross-questioning me, attempting to draw from me information unawares. I thought it advisable to be on my guard.

"On the contrary," said I, "I bolted my door."

"Then you are not in the habit of bolting your door every night before you get into bed?"

## Chapter 16

Fiend! she wants to know my habits, that she may lay her plans accordingly!

I replied sharply, "I was not aware any danger was to be dreaded at Thornfield Hall, but in future I shall take good care to make all secure before I lie down."

"It will be wise so to do," was her answer. "I always think it best to err on the safe side; a door is soon fastened and it is as well to have a drawn bolt between one and any mischief that may be about."

I still stood absolutely dumfoundered at what appeared to me her miraculous self-possession when the cook entered.

"Mrs Poole," said she, addressing Grace, "the servants' dinner will soon be ready; will you come down?"

"No, just put my pint of porter and bit of pudding on a tray and I'll carry it upstairs."

The cook here turned to me, saying that Mrs Fairfax was waiting for me, so I departed.

I hardly heard Mrs Fairfax during dinner, so much was I occupied in puzzling my brains over Grace Poole, and still more in questioning why she had not been given into custody that morning, or, at the very least, dismissed from her master's service. He had almost as much as declared his conviction of her criminality last night: what mysterious cause withheld him from accusing her?

Had Grace been young and handsome, I should have been tempted to think that tenderer feelings than fear influenced Mr Rochester in her behalf, but Mrs Poole's square, flat figure and dry, even coarse face, recurred so distinctly to my mind's eye that I thought, "No, impossible! My supposition cannot be correct. Yet," suggested the secret voice which talks to us in our own hearts, "you are not beautiful either and you have often felt as if Mr Rochester approves you, and last night – remember his words; remember his look; remember his voice!"

I well remembered all: language, glance, and tone seemed at the moment vividly renewed. I was now in the schoolroom; Adèle was drawing; I bent over her and directed her pencil.

"Evening approaches," said I, as I looked towards the window. "I have never heard Mr Rochester's voice or step in the house to-day, but surely I shall see him before night."

When dusk actually closed, and when Adèle left me to go and play in the nursery with Sophie, I did most keenly desire it. I listened for the bell to ring below; I fancied sometimes I heard Mr Rochester's own tread, and I turned to the door, expecting it to open and admit him. The door remained shut. Still, it was not late; he often sent for me at seven and eight o'clock and it was yet but six. Surely, I should not be wholly disappointed to-night, when I had so many things to say to him!

A tread creaked on the stairs at last. Leah made her appearance, but it was only to intimate that tea was ready in Mrs Fairfax's room. Thither I repaired, glad at least to go downstairs for that brought me, I imagined, nearer to Mr Rochester's presence.

"You must want your tea," said the good lady, as I joined her. "You ate so little at dinner. I am afraid," she continued, "you are not well to-day: you look flushed and feverish."

"Oh, quite well! I never felt better."

Having completed her knitting, she rose to draw down the blind.

"It is fair to-night," said she, as she looked through the panes. "Rochester has, on the whole, had a favourable day for his journey."

"Journey! Is Mr Rochester gone anywhere?"

"Oh, he set off the moment he had breakfasted! He is gone to the Leas, Mr Eshton's place, ten miles on the other side of Millcote. I believe there is quite a party assembled there."

"Do you expect him back to-night?"

"No – nor to-morrow either; I should think he is very likely to stay a week or more. Gentlemen, especially, are often in request on such occasions, and Mr Rochester is a general favourite: the ladies are very fond of him, though you would not think his appearance calculated to recommend him particularly in their eyes."

"Are there ladies at the Leas?"

## Chapter 16

"There are the Honourable Blanche and Mary Ingram, most beautiful women. Indeed, I have seen Blanche; she came here to a Christmas ball and party Mr Rochester gave. You should have seen the dining-room that day – how richly it was decorated, how brilliantly lit up! Miss Ingram was considered the belle of the evening."

"You saw her, you say, Mrs Fairfax: what was she like?"

"Yes, the ladies were magnificently dressed. Most of them – at least most of the younger ones – looked handsome, but Miss Ingram was certainly the queen; tall, with a fine bust; sloping shoulders; long, graceful neck; olive complexion, dark and clear; noble features; eyes rather like Mr Rochester's: large and black, and as brilliant as her jewels. And then she had such a fine head of hair – raven-black and so becomingly arranged: a crown of thick plaits and the glossiest curls I ever saw. She was dressed in pure white."

"She was greatly admired, of course?"

"Yes, indeed, and not only for her beauty, but for her accomplishments. She was one of the ladies who sang: a gentleman accompanied her on the piano. She and Mr Rochester sang a duet."

"Mr Rochester? I was not aware he could sing."

"Oh! He has a fine bass voice and an excellent taste for music."

"And Miss Ingram: what sort of a voice had she?"

"A very rich and powerful one; she sang delightfully."

"And this beautiful and accomplished lady, she is not yet married?"

"It appears not: I fancy neither she nor her sister have very large fortunes."

At that moment, Adèle came in and the conversation was turned into another channel.

When once more alone, I looked into my heart, examined its thoughts and feelings, and endeavoured to bring back with a strict hand common sense.

I pronounced judgment to this effect:

That a greater fool than Jane Eyre had never breathed the breath of life; that a more fantastic idiot had never indulged in sweet lies and swallowed poison as if it were nectar.

"*You*," I said, "a favourite with Mr Rochester? *You* gifted with the power of pleasing him? *You* of importance to him in any way? Go! Your folly sickens me. And you have derived pleasure from occasional tokens of preference. How dared you? Poor stupid dupe! You repeated to yourself this morning the brief scene of last night? Cover your face and be ashamed! He said something in praise of your eyes, did he? Blind puppy! It does good to no woman to be flattered by her superior, who cannot possibly intend to marry her, and it is madness in all women to let a secret love kindle within them.

"Listen, then, Jane Eyre, to your sentence: to-morrow, place the glass before you and draw in chalk your own picture, faithfully, without softening one defect. Write under it, 'Portrait of a Governess, disconnected, poor, and plain.'

"Afterwards, take a piece of smooth ivory: take your palette, mix your freshest, finest, clearest tints; choose your most delicate pencils; delineate carefully the loveliest face you can imagine, according to the description given by Mrs Fairfax of Blanche Ingram. No snivel! No sentiment! No regret! I will endure only sense and resolution. Recall dazzling arm and the delicate hand; omit neither diamond ring nor gold bracelet. Call it, 'Blanche, an accomplished lady of rank.'

"Whenever, in future, you should chance to fancy Mr Rochester thinks well of you, take out these two pictures and compare them. Say, 'Mr Rochester might probably win that noble lady's love, if he chose to strive for it; is it likely he would waste a serious thought on this insignificant fool?'"

"I'll do it," I resolved, and having framed this determination, I grew calm, and fell asleep.

# Chapter 17

Mr Rochester had been absent a fortnight and I was permitting myself to experience a sickening sense of disappointment when the post brought Mrs Fairfax a letter. "It is from the master," said she, as she looked at the address. "Now I suppose we shall know whether we are to expect his return or not."

While she broke the seal and perused the document, a fiery glow suddenly rose to my face. "You have nothing to do with the master of Thornfield," I said to myself. "He is not of your order: keep to your level."

"Well, I sometimes think we are too quiet, but we run a chance of being busy enough now, for a little while at least," said Mrs Fairfax, still holding the note before her spectacles.

"Mr Rochester is not likely to return soon, I suppose?" I said, nonchalantly.

"Indeed he is – in three days, and not alone either. I don't know how many fine people are coming with him: he sends directions for all the best bedrooms to be prepared; we shall have a full house of it." And Mrs Fairfax swallowed her breakfast and hastened away to commence operations.

The three days were, as she had foretold, busy enough. Three women were got to help and such scrubbing, such brushing, such lighting of fires in bedrooms, I never beheld, either before or since. From school duties I was exonerated: Mrs Fairfax had pressed me into her service, and I was all day helping the cook, learning to make custards and cheese-cakes and French pastry.

Still, now and then, I chanced to see the third-storey staircase door (which of late had always been kept locked) open slowly and give passage to the form of Grace Poole gliding along the gallery. Only one hour in the twenty-four did she pass with her fellow-servants below; all the rest of her time was spent in some low-ceiled, oaken chamber of the second storey: there she sat and sewed – and probably laughed drearily to herself – as companionless as a prisoner in his dungeon.

The strangest thing was that not a soul in the house, except me, noticed her habits or seemed to marvel at them. I once, indeed, overheard part of a dialogue between Leah and one of the charwomen, of which Grace formed the subject. Leah had been saying something I had not caught, and the charwoman remarked –

"She gets good wages, I guess?"

"Yes," said Leah, "I wish I had as good; they're not one fifth of the sum Mrs Poole receives. I should not wonder but she has saved enough to keep her independent if she liked to leave."

"Ah! She understands what she has to do," said the charwoman significantly, "and it is not everyone could fill her shoes – not for all the money she gets."

"That it is not!" was the reply.

The charwoman was going on but here Leah turned and perceived me, and she instantly gave her companion a nudge.

"Doesn't she know?" I heard the woman whisper.

Leah shook her head and the conversation was of course dropped. All I had gathered from it amounted to this – that there was a mystery at Thornfield, and that from participation in that mystery I was purposely excluded.

Thursday afternoon arrived: Mrs Fairfax assumed her best black satin gown, her gloves, and her gold watch, for it was her part to receive the company.

It had been a mild, serene spring day – it was drawing to an end now but the evening was warm, and I sat at work in the schoolroom with the window open.

## Chapter 17

"It gets late," said Mrs Fairfax, entering in rustling state. "I am glad I ordered dinner an hour after the time Mr Rochester mentioned, for it is past six now."

At last wheels were heard; four equestrians galloped up the drive, and after them came two open carriages. Mr Rochester rode on his black horse; at his side rode a lady, and he and she were the first of the party. Her purple riding-habit almost swept the ground, and her veil streamed long on the breeze.

"Miss Ingram!" exclaimed Mrs Fairfax, and away she hurried to her post below.

A joyous stir was now audible in the hall. Then light steps ascended the stairs and there was a tripping through the gallery and soft cheerful laughs and opening and closing doors, and, for a time, a hush.

Presently the chambers gave up their fair tenants one after another: each came out gaily and airily, with dress that gleamed lustrous through the dusk. Their collective appearance had left on me an impression of high-born elegance, such as I had never before received.

The next day was as fine as its predecessor; it was devoted by the party to an excursion to some site in the neighbourhood. They set out early in the forenoon, some on horseback, the rest in carriages; I witnessed both the departure and the return. Miss Ingram, as before, was the only lady equestrian, and, as before, Mr Rochester galloped at her side; the two rode a little apart from the rest. I pointed out this circumstance to Mrs Fairfax, who was standing at the window with me –

"You said it was not likely they should think of being married," said I, "but you see Mr Rochester evidently prefers her to any of the other ladies."

"Yes, I daresay: no doubt he admires her."

"And she him," I added. "Look how she leans her head towards him as if she were conversing confidentially; I wish I could see her face; I have never had a glimpse of it yet."

"You will see her this evening," answered Mrs Fairfax. "I happened to remark to Mr Rochester how much Adèle wished to be introduced to the ladies, and he said: 'Oh! Let her come into the drawing-room after dinner, and request Miss Eyre to accompany her. If she objects, tell her it is my particular wish, and if she resists, say I shall come and fetch her.'"

"I will not give him that trouble," I answered. "I will go, but I don't like it."

It was with some trepidation that I perceived the hour approach when I was to repair to the drawing-room. Adèle had been in a state of ecstasy all day, after hearing she was to be presented to the ladies in the evening, and it was not till Sophie commenced the operation of dressing her that she sobered down. Then the importance of the process quickly steadied her and by the time she had her curls arranged, her pink satin frock put on, and her lace mittens adjusted, she looked as grave as any judge. My best dress was soon put on; my hair was soon smoothed. We descended to the drawing-room and found the apartment vacant; a large fire burning silently on the marble hearth.

Adèle sat down without a word. I retired to a window-seat, and taking a book from a table near, endeavoured to read. A soft sound of rising now became audible; the curtain was swept back from the arch; through it appeared the dining-room. There were but eight; yet, somehow, as they flocked in, they gave the impression of a much larger number. I rose and curtseyed to them: one or two bent their heads in return, while the others only stared at me.

They dispersed about the room, reminding me, by the lightness and buoyancy of their movements, of a flock of white plumy birds. The three most distinguished were the Lady Ingram and her daughters, who were straight and tall as poplars. I regarded Blanche, of course, with special interest. I wished to see whether her appearance were such as I should fancy likely to suit Mr Rochester's taste.

As far as person went, she answered point for point, both to my picture and Mrs Fairfax's description. The noble bust, the sloping shoulders, the graceful neck, the dark eyes and black ringlets were all there. Though she laughed continually, her laugh was satirical, and so was the habitual expression of her arched and haughty lip.

# Chapter 17

And did I now think Miss Ingram such a choice as Mr Rochester would be likely to make? I could not tell – I did not know his taste in female beauty. If he liked the majestic, she was the very type of majesty; she was accomplished – she sang, she talked French and she talked it well. Most gentlemen would admire her, I thought. When the ladies entered, Adèle rose, advanced to meet them, and said with gravity –

"Bonjour, mesdames."

Miss Ingram looked down at her with a mocking air, and exclaimed, "Oh, what a little puppet!"

And then they called her to a sofa, where she now sat, ensconced between them, chattering alternately in French and broken English.

At last coffee is brought in and the gentlemen are summoned. I sit in the shade – the window-curtain half hides me. Mr Rochester comes in last. I wish to think only of the work I have in my hands, to see only the silver beads and silk threads that lie in my lap; whereas, I distinctly behold his figure, and I inevitably recall the moment when I last saw it; just after I had rendered him, what he deemed, an essential service, and he, holding my hand, and looking down on my face, surveyed me with eyes that revealed a heart full and eager to overflow, in whose emotions I had a part. How near had I approached him at that moment! Yet now, how distant, how far estranged we were! So far estranged, that I did not expect him to come and speak to me. I did not wonder, when, without looking at me, he took a seat at the other side of the room and began conversing with some of the ladies.

Most true is it that "beauty is in the eye of the gazer." My master's face, square brow, strong features, firm, grim mouth, were not beautiful, according to rule, but they were more than beautiful to me.

Coffee is handed. The ladies, since the gentlemen entered, have become lively as larks; conversation waxes brisk and merry. Colonel Dent and Mr Eshton argue on politics; their wives listen. Lady Lynn and Lady Ingram gossip together. With whom will Blanche Ingram pair? She is standing alone at the table, bending gracefully over an album. Mr Rochester stands on the hearth as solitary as she stands by the table: she confronts him, taking her station on the opposite side of the mantelpiece.

"Mr Rochester, I thought you were not fond of children?"

"Nor am I."

"Then, what induced you to take charge of such a little doll as that?" (pointing to Adèle). "You should have sent her to school."

"I could not afford it: schools are so dear."

"Why, I suppose you have a governess for her: I saw a person with her just now – there she is still, behind the window-curtain. You pay her, of course; I should think it quite as expensive."

I feared – or should I say, hoped? – the allusion to me would make Mr Rochester glance my way, but he never turned his eyes.

"I have not considered the subject," said he indifferently, looking straight before him.

"You should hear mama on the chapter of governesses. Mary and I have had, I should think, a dozen at least in our day, half of them detestable and the rest ridiculous – were they not, mama?"

"My dearest, don't mention governesses; the word makes me nervous. I thank Heaven I have now done with them!"

"I have just one word to say of the whole tribe," cried Blanche, "they are a nuisance. Not that I ever suffered much from governesses. What tricks Theodore and I used to play on ours! Theodore, do you remember those merry days?"

"Yaas, to be sure I do," drawled Lord Ingram, "and the poor old sticks used to cry out, 'Oh you villains!'"

"They did!" cried Blanche, tossing her head with all its curls, as she moved to the piano. Having had now seated herself with proud grace at the piano, she spread out her snowy robes and commenced a brilliant prelude, talking meantime. Both her words and her air seemed intended to excite not only the admiration, but the amazement of her auditors:

she was evidently bent on striking them as something very dashing and daring indeed.

"Oh, I am so sick of the young men of the present day!" exclaimed she, rattling away at the instrument. "Poor, puny things! Creatures so absorbed in care about their pretty faces; as if a man had anything to do with beauty! I grant an ugly woman is a blot on the fair face of creation; but as to the gentlemen, let them possess only strength and valour; let their motto be: hunt, shoot, and fight. Such should be my device, were I a man. Mr Rochester, now sing, and I will play for you."

"I am all obedience," was the response.

"Now is my time to slip away," thought I and made my exit by the side-door. Thence a narrow passage led into the hall. I heard the dining-room door unclose; a gentleman came out; it was Mr Rochester.

"How do you do?" he asked.

"I am very well, sir."

"Why did you not come and speak to me in the room?"

"I did not wish to disturb you, as you seemed engaged, sir."

"What have you been doing during my absence?"

"Nothing particular; teaching Adèle as usual."

"And getting a good deal paler than you were – as I saw at first sight. What is the matter?"

"Nothing at all, sir."

"Did you take any cold that night you half drowned me?"

"Not the least."

"Return to the drawing-room: you are deserting too early."

"I am tired, sir."

He looked at me for a minute.

"And a little depressed," he said. "What about? Tell me."

"Nothing – nothing, sir. I am not depressed."

"But I affirm that you are: so much depressed that a few more words would bring tears to your eyes – indeed, they are there now. If I had time, and was not in mortal dread of some servant passing, I would know what all this means. Well, to-night I excuse you, but understand that so long as my visitors stay, I expect you to appear in the drawing-room every evening. It is my wish; don't neglect it. Now go. Good-night, my—" He stopped, bit his lip, and abruptly left me.

# Chapter 18

Merry days were these at Thornfield Hall, and busy days too: how different from the first three months of stillness, monotony, and solitude I had passed beneath its roof! There was life everywhere, movement all day long. Even when the fine weather was broken and continuous rain set in for some days, no damp seemed cast over enjoyment; indoor amusements only became more lively and varied.

I wondered what they were going to do the first evening a change of entertainment was proposed; they spoke of "playing charades". The servants were called in, the dining-room tables wheeled away.

Meantime, Mr Rochester had again summoned the ladies round him and was selecting certain of their number to be of his party. "Miss Ingram is mine, of course," said he. Afterwards, he named the two Misses Eshton, and Mrs Dent. He looked at me: I happened to be near him, as I had been fastening the clasp of Mrs Dent's bracelet, which had got loose.

"Will you play?" he asked. I shook my head. He did not insist, which I rather feared he would have done.

"No," I heard Lady Ingram say, "she looks too stupid for any game of the sort."

As the first party withdrew to prepare their charade, Miss Ingram placed herself at Mr Rochester's right hand. What charade Colonel Dent and his party played, I no longer remember, but I still see Mr Rochester turn to Miss Ingram, and Miss Ingram to him; I see her incline her head towards him; I hear their mutual whisperings; I recall their interchanged glances.

I had learnt to love Mr Rochester: I could not unlove him now, merely because I found that he had ceased to notice me – because I might pass hours in his presence and he would never once turn his eyes in my direction. I could not unlove him, because I felt sure he would soon marry this very lady.

But I was not jealous, or very rarely. Miss Ingram was a mark beneath jealousy: she was too inferior to excite the feeling. She was very showy but she was not genuine: she had a fine person, many brilliant attainments, but her mind was poor. She was not good; she was not original; she never offered, nor had, an opinion of her own.

I saw he was going to marry her, for family, perhaps political reasons, because her rank and connections suited him, but I felt he had not given her his love. This was the point: she could not charm him.

If Miss Ingram had been a good and noble woman, endowed with force, fervour, kindness, sense, I should have struggled with jealousy and despair. But as matters really stood, to watch Miss Ingram's efforts at fascinating Mr Rochester, to witness their repeated failure – herself unconscious that they did fail – to witness *this*, was to be at once under ceaseless excitation and ruthless restraint.

Because, when she failed, I saw how she might have succeeded.

I have not yet said anything condemnatory of Mr Rochester's project of marrying for interest and connections. It surprised me when I first discovered that such was his intention, but the longer I considered the position and education of the parties, the less I felt justified in judging and blaming either him or Miss Ingram for ideas instilled into them, doubtless, from their childhood. All their class held these principles.

One day he had been summoned to Millcote on business and was not likely to return till late. The afternoon was wet: a walk the party had proposed was deferred. Some of the gentlemen were gone to the stables; the younger ones, together with the younger ladies, were playing billiards in the billiard-room. The ladies sought solace in a quiet game at cards. The room and the house were silent; only now and then the merriment of the billiard-players was heard from above.

It was verging on dusk when a crunching of wheels and a splashing tramp of horse-hoofs became audible on the wet gravel. A post-chaise was approaching.

## Chapter 18

It stopped; the driver rang the door-bell, and a gentleman alighted attired in travelling garb, but it was not Mr Rochester; it was a tall, fashionable-looking man, a stranger.

Some parleying was audible in the hall, and soon the new-comer entered. He bowed to Lady Ingram, as deeming her the eldest lady present.

"I arrive from a very long journey," said he, "and I think I may presume so far on old and intimate acquaintance as to install myself here till Mr Rochester returns."

His manner was polite; his accent, in speaking, struck me as being somewhat unusual – not precisely foreign, but still not altogether English; his age might be about Mr Rochester's – between thirty and forty.

It was not till after dinner that I saw him again. His eye wandered and had no meaning in its wandering: this gave him an odd look, such as I never remembered to have seen.

He had spoken of Mr Rochester as an old friend. A curious friendship theirs must have been.

I presently gathered that the new-comer was called Mr Mason; then I learned that he was but just arrived in England, and that he came from Jamaica – the West Indies was his residence and I gathered, ere long, that he had there first seen and become acquainted with Mr Rochester.

I was pondering these things, when an incident, and a somewhat unexpected one, broke the thread of my musings. The footman, who was bringing more coal for the fire, stopped near Mr Eshton's chair, and said something to him in a low voice, of which I heard only the words, "old woman," – "quite troublesome."

"Tell her she shall be put in the stocks if she does not take herself off," he replied.

"No – stop!" interrupted Colonel Dent. "Don't send her away." And speaking aloud, he continued – "Ladies, Sam here says that a gypsy is in the servants' hall at this moment. Would you like to see her?"

"What does she want?" asked Mrs Eshton.

"'To tell the gentry their fortunes,' she says, ma'am, and she swears she must and will do it."

"What is she like?" inquired the Misses Eshton, in a breath.

"A shockingly ugly old creature."

"Why, she's a real sorceress!" cried Frederick Lynn. "Let us have her in, of course."

Excitement instantly seized the whole party: a running fire of jests was proceeding when Sam returned.

"She won't come now," said he. "I must show her into a room by herself and then those who wish to consult her must go to her one by one."

"Show her into the library, of course," replied Blanche. "I mean to have her all to myself. Is there a fire in the library?"

"Yes, ma'am."

Again Sam vanished, and mystery, animation, expectation rose to full flow once more.

"She's ready now," said the footman, as he reappeared.

Miss Ingram rose solemnly: "I go first," she said and swept past.

A comparative silence ensued.

The minutes passed very slowly: fifteen were counted before the library-door again opened. Miss Ingram returned to us through the arch.

Would she laugh? Would she take it as a joke? All eyes met her with a glance of eager curiosity, and she met all eyes with one of rebuff and coldness; she looked neither flurried nor merry: she walked stiffly to her seat and took it in silence.

"Well, Blanche?" said Lord Ingram.

"What did she say, sister?" asked Mary.

"Now, now, good people," returned Miss Ingram, "don't press upon me."

Miss Ingram took a book, leant back in her chair, and so declined further conversation. I watched her for nearly half-an-hour: during all that time she never turned a page, and her face grew momently darker and more sourly expressive of disappointment. She had obviously not heard anything to her advantage.

Meantime, Mary Ingram, Amy and Louisa Eshton declared they dared not go alone, and permission was given for the three to wait upon her together.

Their visit was not so still as Miss Ingram's had been: we heard hysterical giggling and little shrieks proceeding from the library and at the end of about twenty minutes they burst the door open and came running across the hall, as if they were half-scared out of their wits.

"I am sure she is something not right!" they cried, one and all. "She told us such things! She knows all about us!" and they sank breathless into the various seats the gentlemen hastened to bring them.

In the midst of the tumult, I heard a hem close at my elbow: I turned, and saw Sam.

"If you please, miss, the gypsy declares that there is another young single lady in the room who has not been to her yet, and she swears she will not go till she has seen all. I thought it must be you: there is no one else for it. What shall I tell her?"

"Oh, I will go by all means," I answered, and I was glad of the unexpected opportunity to gratify my curiosity. I slipped out of the room, unobserved by any eye – for the company were gathered in one mass about the trembling trio just returned – and I closed the door quietly behind me.

"If you like, miss," said Sam, "I'll wait in the hall for you and if she frightens you, just call and I'll come in."

"No, Sam, return to the kitchen: I am not in the least afraid." Nor was I, but I was a good deal interested and excited.

99

# Chapter 19

The library looked tranquil enough as I entered it, and the gypsy was seated snugly enough in an easy-chair at the chimney-corner. She had on a red cloak and a broad-brimmed gypsy hat, tied down with a striped handkerchief under her chin.

I stood on the rug and warmed my hands. I felt now as composed as ever I did in my life; there was nothing indeed in the gypsy's appearance to trouble one's calm. She shut her book and slowly looked up. Her hat-brim partially shaded her face, yet I could see, as she raised it, that it was a strange one. Her eye confronted me at once, with a bold and direct gaze.

"Well, and you want your fortune told?" she said.

"I don't care about it. You may please yourself, but I ought to warn you, I have no faith."

"Why don't you tremble?"

"I'm not cold."

"Why don't you turn pale?"

"I am not sick."

"Why don't you consult my art?"

"I'm not silly."

The old crone laughed under her bonnet. She then drew out a short black pipe, and while gazing steadily at the fire, said very deliberately:

"You are cold; you are sick; and you are silly."

"Prove it," I rejoined.

## Chapter 19

"I will, in few words. You are cold, because you are alone. No contact strikes the fire from you that is in you. You are sick because the best of feelings, the highest and the sweetest given to man, keeps far away from you. You are silly because, suffer as you may, you will not beckon it to approach, nor will you stir one step to meet it where it waits you."

She again put her short black pipe to her lips and began her smoking with vigour.

"You might say all that to almost anyone who you knew lived as a solitary dependent in a great house."

"I might say it to almost anyone, but would it be true of almost anyone?"

"In my circumstances."

"Kneel, and lift up your head," she commanded.

I knelt within half a yard of her. She stirred the fire, so that a ripple of light broke from the disturbed coal. The glare, however, as she sat, only threw her face into deeper shadow; mine, it illumined.

"I wonder with what feelings you came to me to-night," she said, when she had examined me a while. "I wonder what thoughts are busy in your heart during all the hours you sit in yonder room with the fine people flitting before you like shapes in a magic-lantern."

"I feel tired often, sleepy sometimes, but seldom sad."

"Then you have some secret hope to buoy you up and please you with whispers of the future?"

"Not I. The utmost I hope is to save money enough out of my earnings to set up a school some day in a little house rented by myself."

"Sitting in that window-seat, do you think of nothing but your future school? Have you no present interest in any of the company? Is there not one face you study?"

"I like to observe all the faces and all the figures."

"Is it nothing to you when a lady, young and charming with beauty, sits and smiles in the eyes of a gentleman you—"

"I what?"

"You think well of."

"I don't know the gentlemen here. I have scarcely interchanged a syllable with one of them."

"You don't know the gentlemen here? You have not exchanged a syllable with one of them? Will you say that of the master of the house!"

"He is not at home."

"A profound remark! A most ingenious quibble!"

"I can scarcely see what Mr Rochester has to do with the theme you had introduced."

"I was talking of ladies smiling in the eyes of gentlemen, and of late many smiles have been shed into Mr Rochester's eyes."

"Mr Rochester has a right to enjoy the society of his guests."

"Mr Rochester will shortly be married to the beautiful Miss Ingram and, no doubt, they will be a superlatively happy pair. He must love such a handsome, noble, witty, accomplished lady, and probably she loves him, or, if not his person, at least his purse. Though I told her something on that point about an hour ago which made her look wondrous grave; the corners of her mouth fell half an inch."

"But I did not come to hear Mr Rochester's fortune, I came to hear my own, and you have told me nothing of it."

"Your fortune is yet doubtful. Chance has meted you a measure of happiness – that I know. It depends on yourself to stretch out your hand and take it up, but whether you will do so, is the problem I study."

She began muttering:

"The flame flickers in the eye; the eye shines like dew; it looks soft and full of feeling; it smiles at my jargon. As to the mouth, it delights at times in laughter.

"I see no enemy to a fortunate issue but in the brow. And that brow professes to say: 'Reason sits firm and holds the reins, and she will not let the feelings burst away. I have formed my plans – right plans I deem them.'

"That will do. I think I rave in a kind of exquisite delirium. I should wish now to protract this moment ad infinitum, but I dare not. I have acted as I inwardly swore I would act, but further might try me beyond my strength. Rise, Miss Eyre – leave me."

Had I been dreaming? Did I dream still? The old woman's voice had changed. Her accent, her gesture, and all, were familiar to me as my own face in a glass – as the speech of my own tongue. I got up, but did not go.

"Well, Jane, do you know me?" asked the familiar voice.

Mr Rochester stepped out of his disguise.

"Now, sir, what a strange idea!"

"But well carried out, eh? Don't you think so?"

"With the ladies you must have managed well."

"But not with you?"

"You did not act the character of a gypsy with me."

"Do you forgive me, Jane?"

"I cannot tell till I have thought it all over."

"Oh, you have been very correct – very careful, very sensible."

I reflected, and thought, on the whole, I had. It was a comfort, but, indeed, I had been on my guard almost from the beginning of the interview.

"I had better not stay long, sir. It must be near eleven o'clock. Oh, are you aware, Mr Rochester, that a stranger has arrived here since you left this morning?"

"A stranger! No. Who can it be? I expected no one. Is he gone?"

"No. He said he had known you long, and that he could take the liberty of installing himself here till you returned."

"The devil he did! Did he give his name?"

"His name is Mason, sir, and he comes from the West Indies; from Spanish Town, in Jamaica, I think."

Mr Rochester was standing near me. He had taken my hand, as if to lead me to a chair. As I spoke he gave my wrist a convulsive grip. The smile on his lips froze.

"Mason! The West Indies!" he said, whiter than ashes. He hardly seemed to know what he was doing.

"Do you feel ill, sir?" I inquired.

"Jane, I've got a blow. I've got a blow, Jane!" He staggered.

"Oh, lean on me, sir."

"Jane, you offered me your shoulder once before; let me have it now."

"Yes, sir, yes, and my arm."

He sat down, and made me sit beside him. Holding my hand in both his own, he chafed it, gazing on me, at the same time, with the most troubled and dreary look.

"I wish I were in a quiet island with only you – and trouble, and danger, and hideous recollections removed from me."

"Can I help you, sir? I'd give my life to serve you."

"Jane, if aid is wanted, I'll seek it at your hands. I promise you that."

"Thank you, sir. Tell me what to do – I'll try, at least, to do it."

"Fetch me now, Jane, a glass of wine from the dining-room. They will be at supper there – tell me if Mason is with them, and what he is doing."

I went. I found all the party in the dining-room at supper, as Mr Rochester had said. I filled a wine-glass and I returned to the library.

Mr Rochester's extreme pallor had disappeared, and he looked once more firm and stern. He took the glass from my hand.

"Here is to your health!" he said. He swallowed the contents and returned it to me. "What are they doing, Jane?"

"Laughing and talking, sir."

"They don't look grave and mysterious, as if they had heard something strange?"

"Not at all."

"And Mason?"

"He was laughing too."

"If all these people came in a body and spat at me, what would you do, Jane?"

"Turn them out of the room, sir, if I could."

He half smiled. "But if I were to go to them, and they only looked at me coldly, and whispered sneeringly amongst each other, and then dropped off and left me one by one, what then? Would you go with them?"

"I rather think not, sir. I should have more pleasure in staying with you."

"To comfort me?"

"Yes, sir, to comfort you, as well as I could."

"Go back now into the room. Step quietly up to Mason, and whisper in his ear that Mr Rochester is come and wishes to see him. Show him in here and then leave me."

"Yes, sir."

I did his behest. The company all stared at me as I passed straight among them. I sought Mr Mason, delivered the message, and preceded him from the room. I ushered him into the library, and then I went upstairs.

At a late hour, after I had been in bed some time, I heard the visitors repair to their chambers. I distinguished Mr Rochester's voice, and heard him say, "This way, Mason; this is your room."

He spoke cheerfully. The gay tones set my heart at ease. I was soon asleep.

# Chapter 20

I had forgotten to draw my curtain and, awaking in the dead of night, I opened my eyes on the full moon – silver-white and crystal clear. It was beautiful, but too solemn. I half rose, and stretched my arm to draw the curtain.

Good God! What a cry!

The night – its silence – its rest, was rent in twain by a savage, a sharp, sound that ran from end to end of Thornfield Hall.

My pulse stopped; my heart stood still; my stretched arm was paralysed. The cry died, and was not renewed.

It came out of the third storey, for it passed overhead. And overhead I now heard a struggle: a deadly one it seemed from the noise, and a half-smothered voice shouted –

"Help! Help! Help!" three times rapidly. "Will no one come?" it cried, and then, "Rochester! Rochester! For God's sake, come!"

A chamber-door opened; someone ran, or rushed, along the gallery. Another step stamped on the flooring above and there was silence.

I had put on some clothes, though horror shook all my limbs; I issued from my apartment. The sleepers were all roused; terrified murmurs sounded. Gentlemen and ladies alike had quitted their beds, and "Oh! what is it?" – "Who is hurt?" – "What has happened?" – "Fetch a light!" – "Is it fire?" was demanded confusedly on all hands. But for the moonlight they would have been in complete darkness.

"Where the devil is Rochester?" cried Colonel Dent. "I cannot find him in his bed."

## Chapter 20

"Here! Here!" was shouted in return. "Be composed, all of you – I'm coming."

And the door at the end of the gallery opened, and Mr Rochester advanced with a candle; he had just descended from the upper storey.

"All's right! All's right!" he cried. Calming himself by an effort, he added –

"A servant has had the nightmare, that is all. Now, then, I must see you all back into your rooms for, till the house is settled, she cannot be looked after."

And so, by coaxing and commanding, he contrived to get them all once more enclosed in their separate dormitories. I did not wait to be ordered back to mine, but retreated unnoticed. Not, however, to go to bed; on the contrary, I dressed myself carefully. The sounds I had heard after the scream, and the words that had been uttered, had probably been heard only by me, for they had proceeded from the room above mine, but they assured me that it was not a servant's dream which had thus struck horror through the house, and that the explanation Mr Rochester had given was merely an invention framed to pacify his guests. I dressed, then, to be ready for emergencies.

Stillness returned. Each murmur and movement ceased gradually, and in about an hour Thornfield Hall was again hushed. A cautious hand tapped low at the door.

"Are you up?" asked the voice I expected to hear.

"Yes, sir."

"And dressed?"

"Yes."

"Come out, then, quietly."

I obeyed. Mr Rochester stood in the gallery holding a light.

"I want you," he said, "come this way; make no noise."

He glided up the gallery and up the stairs, and stopped in the dark, low corridor of the fateful third storey; I had followed and stood at his side.

"Have you a sponge in your room?" he asked in a whisper.

"Yes, sir."

"Go back and fetch it."

I returned, sought the sponge on the washstand and once more retraced my steps. He still waited; he held a key in his hand. Approaching one of the small, black doors, he put it in the lock; he paused, and addressed me again.

"You don't turn sick at the sight of blood?"

"I think I shall not."

I felt a thrill while I answered him, but no faintness.

"Just give me your hand," he said, "it will not do to risk a fainting fit."

I put my fingers into his. He turned the key and opened the door.

I saw a room I remembered to have seen before, the day Mrs Fairfax showed me over the house. It was hung with tapestry, but the tapestry was now looped up in one part, and there was a door which had then been concealed. This door was open; a light shone out of the room within; I heard thence a snarling, snatching sound, almost like a dog. Mr Rochester went forward to the inner apartment. A shout of laughter greeted his entrance, noisy at first, and terminating in Grace Poole's own goblin ha! ha! *She* then was there. He made some sort of arrangement without speaking, though I heard a low voice address him. He came out and closed the door behind him.

"Here, Jane!" he said, and I walked round to the other side of a large bed. An easy-chair was near the bed-head; a man sat in it; he was still; his head leant back; his eyes were closed. Mr Rochester held the candle over him. I recognised in his pale and seemingly lifeless face – the stranger, Mason. I saw too that his linen on one side, and one arm, was almost soaked in blood.

"Hold the candle," said Mr Rochester, and I took it. He fetched a basin of water. "Hold that," said he. I obeyed. He took the sponge, dipped it in, and moistened the corpse-like face. Mr Mason shortly unclosed his eyes; he groaned. Mr Rochester opened the shirt of the wounded man, whose

# Chapter 20

arm and shoulder were bandaged. He sponged away blood, trickling fast down.

"Is there immediate danger?" murmured Mr Mason.

"Pooh! No – a mere scratch. I'll fetch a surgeon for you now, myself. You'll be able to be removed by morning, I hope. Jane," he continued.

"Sir?"

"I shall have to leave you in this room with this gentleman, for an hour, or perhaps two hours. You will sponge the blood as I do when it returns. You will not speak to him on any pretext – and – Richard, it will be at the peril of your life if you speak to her."

Again the poor man groaned. Mr Rochester put the now bloody sponge into my hand, and I proceeded to use it as he had done. He watched me a second, then saying, "Remember! No conversation," he left the room. I experienced a strange feeling as the key grated in the lock, and the sound of his retreating step ceased to be heard.

Here then I was in the third storey, night around me, a pale and bloody spectacle under my eyes and hands, a murderess hardly separated from me by a single door. I shuddered at the thought of Grace Poole bursting out upon me. I must keep to my post, however. I must watch this ghastly countenance – these blue, still lips forbidden to unclose – these eyes now shut, now opening, and ever glazed with the dullness of horror. I must dip my hand again and again in the basin of blood and water, and wipe away the trickling gore. I must see the light of the unsnuffed candle wane on my employment, the shadows darken on the tapestry round me and grow black under the hangings of the vast old bed, and quiver strangely over the doors of a great cabinet opposite.

Amidst all this, I had to listen as well as watch; all the night I heard but three sounds at three long intervals: a step creak, a momentary renewal of the snarling, canine noise, and a deep human groan. Then my own thoughts worried me. What creature was it, that, masked in an ordinary woman's face and shape, uttered the voice of a mocking demon? And this man I bent over – this commonplace, quiet stranger – how had he become involved in the web of horror? Why did Mr Rochester enforce this concealment?

"When will he come? When will he come?" I cried inwardly, as the night lingered and lingered – as my bleeding patient drooped, moaned, sickened, and neither day nor aid arrived. He moaned so, and looked so weak, wild, and lost, I feared he was dying; and I might not even speak to him.

The candle, wasted at last, went out. As it expired, I perceived streaks of grey light edging the window curtains; dawn was then approaching. Presently I heard Pilot bark far below. In five minutes more the grating key warned me my watch was relieved.

Mr Rochester entered, and with him the surgeon he had been to fetch.

"Now, Carter, be on the alert," he said to this last. "I give you but half-an-hour for dressing the wound, fastening the bandages, getting the patient downstairs and all."

"But is he fit to move, sir?"

"No doubt of it; it is nothing serious. Come, set to work."

Mr Rochester drew back the thick curtain, let in all the daylight he could, and I was surprised to see how far dawn was advanced. Then he approached Mason, whom the surgeon was already handling.

"Now, my good fellow, how are you?" he asked.

"She's done for me, I fear," was the faint reply.

"Not a whit! – courage! You've lost a little blood, that's all. Carter, assure him there's no danger."

"I can do that," said Carter, who had now undone the bandages, "but how is this? The flesh on the shoulder is torn as well as cut. This wound was not done with a knife; there have been teeth here!"

"She bit me," he murmured, "when Rochester got the knife from her."

"You should not have yielded; you should have grappled with her at once," said Mr Rochester.

"But what could one do?" returned Mason. "I did not expect it; she looked so quiet at first."

## Chapter 20

"I warned you," was his friend's answer, "I said – be on your guard when you go near her."

"I thought I could have done some good."

"You thought! You thought! Carter – hurry! The sun will soon rise, and I must have him off."

"Directly, sir; the shoulder is just bandaged. I must look to this other wound in the arm. She has had her teeth here too, I think."

"She sucked the blood. She said she'd drain my heart," said Mason.

I saw Mr Rochester shudder, but he only said: "Come, be silent, Richard, don't repeat it."

"I wish I could forget it," was the answer.

"You will when you are out of the country. When you get back to Spanish Town, you may think of her as dead and buried.

"Jane," (he turned to me), "go down into my bedroom, and take out a clean shirt and neck-handkerchief. Bring them here."

I went, found the articles named, and returned with them.

"Was anybody stirring below when you went down, Jane?" inquired Mr Rochester presently.

"No, sir; all was very still."

Mr Mason was dressed now. He still looked pale, but he was no longer gory and sullied. Mr Rochester took his arm –

"Now I am sure you can get on your feet," he said, "try."

The patient rose.

"Now, Jane, trip on before us away to the backstairs; unbolt the side-passage door, and tell the driver of the post-chaise you will see in the yard to be ready; we are coming."

It was by this time half-past five, and the sun was on the point of rising, but all the yard was quiet. The gates stood wide open, and there was a post-chaise, with horses ready harnessed, and driver seated on the box.

I approached him, and said the gentlemen were coming. The stillness of early morning slumbered everywhere; little birds were just twittering in the blossom-blanched orchard trees; the carriage horses stamped from time to time. All else was still.

The gentlemen now appeared. Mason, supported by Mr Rochester and the surgeon, seemed to walk with tolerable ease.

"Richard, how is it with you?" asked Mr Rochester.

"The fresh air revives me but—"

"Well, what is it?"

"Let her be taken care of; let her be r—" he stopped and burst into tears.

"I do my best and have done it, and will do it," was the answer. He shut up the chaise door, and the vehicle drove away.

"Yet would to God there was an end of all this!" added Mr Rochester, as he closed and barred the heavy yard-gates.

This done, he moved with slow step towards a door in the wall bordering the orchard.

"Come where there is some freshness, for a few moments," he said, "That house is a mere dungeon; don't you feel it so?"

"It seems to me a splendid mansion, sir."

He strayed down a walk edged with apple trees on one side, and a border on the other full of all sorts of old-fashioned flowers. The sun was just entering the dappled east.

"Jane, will you have a flower?"

He gathered a half-blown rose, the first on the bush, and offered it to me.

"Thank you, sir."

"You have passed a strange night, Jane."

"Yes, sir."

"And it has made you look pale – were you afraid when I left you alone with Mason?"

## Chapter 20

"I was afraid of someone coming out of the inner room."

"But I had fastened the door – I had the key in my pocket; you were safe."

"Will Grace Poole live here still, sir?"

"Oh yes! Don't trouble your head about her – put the thing out of your thoughts."

"Yet it seems to me your life is hardly secure while she stays."

"Never fear – I will take care of myself."

"Is the danger you apprehended last night gone by now, sir?"

"I cannot vouch for that till Mason is out of England, nor even then."

Here, Jane, sit down."

Mr Rochester sat, leaving room, however, for me, but I stood before him.

"Sit," he said, "the bench is long enough for two.

"Now, my little friend, I'll put a case to you. Jane: suppose you were no longer a girl well reared and disciplined, but a wild boy indulged from childhood upwards. Imagine yourself in a remote foreign land; conceive that you there commit a capital error, one whose consequences must follow you through life and taint all your existence. Mind, I don't say a crime; I am not speaking of shedding of blood or any other guilty act. My word is error. The results of what you have done become utterly insupportable; you are miserable, for hope has quitted you. You wander here and there, seeking rest in exile, happiness in heartless, sensual pleasure.

"Heart-weary and soul-withered, you come home after years of voluntary banishment. You make a new acquaintance; you find in this stranger much of the good and bright qualities which you have sought for twenty years, and never before encountered; and they are all fresh, healthy and without taint. Such society revives. You feel better, days come back – you desire to recommence your life. To attain this end, are you justified in overleaping an obstacle of custom – a mere convention? Is the sinful, but now repentant, man justified in daring the world's opinion, in order to attach to him for ever this gentle stranger, thereby securing his own peace of mind and regeneration of life?"

"Sir," I answered, "a sinner's reformation should never depend on a fellow-creature. Let him look higher than his equals for strength to amend."

He paused. The birds went on carolling, the leaves lightly rustling.

"Little friend," said he, in quite a changed, sarcastic tone, "you have noticed Miss Ingram; don't you think if I married her, she would regenerate me?"

He got up suddenly, went quite to the other end of the walk, and when he came back he was humming a tune.

"Jane, Jane," said he, stopping before me, "you are quite pale; don't you curse me for disturbing your rest?"

"No, sir."

"Jane, when will you watch with me again?"

"Whenever I can be useful, sir."

"For instance, the night before I am married! I am sure I shall not be able to sleep. Will you promise to sit up with me to bear me company? Bless me! There's Dent and Lynn in the stables! Go in by the shrubbery, through that wicket."

As I went one way, he went another, and I heard him in the yard, saying cheerfully –

"Mason got the start of you all this morning; he was gone before sunrise. I rose at four to see him off."

# Chapter 21

When I was a little girl, I heard Bessie say that to dream of children was a sure sign of trouble.

During the past week scarcely a night had gone that had not brought with it a dream of an infant. And on the afternoon of the day following, I was summoned downstairs by a message that someone wanted me in Mrs Fairfax's room. I found a man waiting for me, a gentleman's servant, dressed in deep mourning.

"I daresay you hardly remember me, Miss," he said. "I lived coachman with Mrs Reed when you were at Gateshead, and I live there still."

"I remember you very well, Robert. Are the family well at the house?"

"I am sorry I can't give you better news of them, Miss. Mr John died a week ago, at his chambers in London."

"Mr John?"

"Yes."

"And how does his mother bear it?"

"Why, you see, Miss Eyre, these last three years he gave himself up to strange ways, ruined his health and his estate amongst the worst men and the worst women. He got into debt and into jail. How he died, God knows! They say he killed himself."

I was silent; the tidings were frightful. Robert resumed –

"Missis had been out of health herself for some time. The information about Mr John's death and the manner of it came too suddenly: it brought on a stroke. She was three days without speaking, but last Tuesday Bessie made out the words: 'Bring Jane – fetch Jane Eyre; I want to speak to her.'

I left Gateshead yesterday and if you can get ready, Miss, I should like to take you back with me early to-morrow morning."

"Yes, Robert, I shall be ready," and having directed him to the servants' hall, I went in search of Mr Rochester.

He was playing billiards with Miss Ingram. Mr Rochester, Miss Ingram, the two Misses Eshton, and their admirers, were all busied in the game. I approached the master where he stood at Miss Ingram's side.

"Does that person want you?" she inquired of Mr Rochester and Mr Rochester turned to see who the "person" was. He threw down his cue and followed me from the room.

"Well, Jane?" he said.

"If you please, sir, I want leave of absence for a week or two."

"What to do? Where to go?"

"To see Mrs Reed of Gateshead who has sent for me."

"And what have you to do with her?"

"Mr Reed was my uncle – my mother's brother."

"You never told me that before; you always said you had no relations."

"Mr Reed is dead and his wife cast me off."

"You will come back – you will not be induced under any pretext to take up a permanent residence with her?"

"Oh, no! I shall certainly return."

Mr Rochester meditated. "When do you wish to go?"

"Early to-morrow morning, sir."

"Well, you must have some money. I have given you no salary yet. How much have you in the world, Jane?" he asked, smiling.

I drew out my purse. "Five shillings, sir." He took the purse and chuckled over it. "Here," said he, "there are ten pounds. Is it not plenty?"

"Yes, sir, but now you owe me five."

## Chapter 21

"Come back for it, then."

"Mr Rochester, I may as well mention another matter of business to you while I have the opportunity. You have as good as informed me, sir, that you are going shortly to be married?"

"Yes, what then?"

"In that case, sir, Adèle ought to go to school. I must seek another situation somewhere. I shall advertise."

"Jane!"

"Sir?"

"Promise me one thing: not to advertise and to trust this quest of a situation to me. I'll find you one in time."

"I shall be glad so to do, sir, if you, in your turn, will promise that I and Adèle shall be both out of the house before your bride enters it."

"Very well! Very well! I'll pledge my word on it. You go to-morrow, then?"

"Yes, sir, early. Farewell, Mr Rochester, for the present."

"Farewell, Miss Eyre, for the present."

The dinner-bell rang, and suddenly away he bolted, without another syllable. I saw him no more during the day and was off before he had risen in the morning.

I reached Gateshead in the afternoon.

"Bless you! I knew you would come!" exclaimed Bessie, as I entered.

"Yes, Bessie," said I, "and I trust I am not too late. How is Mrs Reed?"

"She is alive and more sensible and collected than she was. The doctor says she may linger a week or two yet. You shall go into the breakfast-room first," said Bessie, as she preceded me through the hall, "the young ladies will be there."

In another moment I was within that apartment. Two young ladies appeared before me: one very tall, very thin too, with a sallow face and severe demeanour. This was Eliza, though I could trace little resemblance to her former self in that elongated and colourless visage. The other was Georgiana, but not the Georgiana I remembered. This was a full-blown, very plump damsel, fair as waxwork, with handsome and regular features, languishing blue eyes, and ringleted yellow hair. Both ladies, as I advanced, rose to welcome me. Eliza's greeting was delivered in a short, abrupt voice without a smile, and then she sat down again, fixed her eyes on the fire, and seemed to forget me. Georgiana added "How d'ye do?" uttered with a coolness of manner. I quietly took off my bonnet and gloves, uninvited, and said I would just step out to Bessie and ask her whether Mrs Reed was disposed to receive me or not to-night.

"Missis is awake," said she. "I have told her you are here: come."

I did not need to be guided to the well-known room, to which I had so often been summoned for chastisement or reprimand in former days. I softly opened the door. I approached the bed; I opened the curtains and leant over the high-piled pillows.

Well did I remember Mrs Reed's face. It is a happy thing that time quells the longings of vengeance and hushes the promptings of rage and aversion. I had left this woman in bitterness and hate, and I came back to her now with no other emotion than a sort of pity for her great sufferings, and a strong yearning to forget and forgive all injuries. I stooped down and kissed her; she looked at me.

"Is this Jane Eyre?" she said.

"Yes, Aunt Reed. How are you, dear aunt?"

I had once vowed that I would never call her aunt again; I thought it no sin to forget and break that vow now. My fingers had fastened on her hand which lay outside the sheet. But Mrs Reed took her hand away and regarded me so icily, that I felt that her feeling towards me was unchanged.

"Are you Jane Eyre?"

"I am Jane Eyre."

"I had more trouble with that child than anyone would believe. Such a burden to be left on my hands – I was glad to get her away from the house. What did they do with her at Lowood? The fever broke out there, and many of the pupils died. She, however, did not die; I wish she had died!

"I had a dislike to her mother always; for she was my husband's only sister, and a great favourite with him, and when news came of her death, he wept like a simpleton. John does not at all resemble his father, and I am glad of it. Oh, I wish he would cease tormenting me with letters for money! I have no more money to give him, for we are getting poor. John gambles dreadfully, and always loses – poor boy!"

She was getting much excited. Bessie now endeavoured to persuade her to take a sedative draught. Soon after, Mrs Reed sank into a dozing state.

More than ten days elapsed before I had again any conversation with her. The rain beat strongly against the panes, and the wind blew tempestuously. "One lies there," I thought, "who will soon be beyond the war of earthly elements."

In pondering that great mystery, I thought of Helen Burns, recalled her dying words – her faith – as she lay on her placid deathbed and whispered her longing to be restored to her divine Father's bosom – when a feeble voice murmured from the couch behind, "Who is that?"

I knew Mrs Reed had not spoken for days. Was she reviving? I went up to her.

"It is I, Aunt Reed."

"Aunt," she repeated. "Who calls me aunt? I know you – that face – why, you are like Jane Eyre! I wished to see Jane Eyre."

I gently assured her that I was the person she supposed me to be, and saw that I was understood, and that her senses were quite collected.

"I am very ill, I know," she said ere long. "It is as well I should ease my mind before I die. Is there no one in the room but you?"

I assured her we were alone.

"Well, I have twice done you a wrong which I regret now. One was in breaking the promise which I gave my husband to bring you up as my own child; the other—" she stopped. "Go to my dressing-case, open it, and take out a letter you will see there."

I obeyed her directions. "Read the letter," she said.

It was short, and thus conceived –

"MADAM,—

Will you have the goodness to send me the address of my niece, Jane Eyre? It is my intention to write and desire her to come to me at Madeira, and as I am unmarried and childless, I wish to adopt her during my life, and bequeath her at my death whatever I may have to leave.

I am, Madam, &c., &c.,

JOHN EYRE, Madeira."

It was dated three years back.

"Why did I never hear of this?" I asked.

"Because I disliked you too fixedly ever to lend a hand in lifting you to prosperity. I could not forget the fury with which you once turned on me, the tone in which you declared you abhorred me the worst of anybody in the world. Bring me some water!"

"Dear Mrs Reed," said I, as I offered her the draught she required, "think no more of all this. Forgive me for my passionate language; years have passed since that day."

"I tell you, I took my revenge. I wrote to your uncle; I said I was sorry for his disappointment, but Jane Eyre was dead. She had died of typhus fever at Lowood."

"Think no more of it, aunt, and regard me with kindness and forgiveness – I long earnestly to be reconciled to you now."

I covered her ice-cold and clammy hand with mine. The feeble fingers shrank from my touch – the glazing eyes shunned my gaze.

"Love me, then, or hate me, as you will," I said at last, "you have my full and free forgiveness."

Poor, suffering woman! It was too late for her to make now the effort to change her habitual frame of mind. Living, she had ever hated me – dying, she must hate me still.

## Chapter 21

At twelve o'clock that night she died. I was not present to close her eyes, nor were either of her daughters. They came to tell us the next morning that all was over. Eliza and I went to look at her; Georgiana, who had burst out into loud weeping, said she dared not go. A strange and solemn object was that corpse to me. I gazed on it with gloom and pain; nothing soft, nothing sweet, nothing pitying, or hopeful, did it inspire. Eliza surveyed her parent calmly. Neither of us had dropped a tear.

# Chapter 22

Mr Rochester had given me but one week's leave of absence, yet a month elapsed before I quitted Gateshead. I wished to leave immediately after the funeral, but Georgiana entreated me to stay till she could get off to London. At last, I saw Georgiana off, but now it was Eliza's turn to request me to stay another week. Her plans required all her time and attention. She wished me to look after the house, to see callers, and answer notes of condolence.

One morning she told me I was free to leave. "To-morrow," she continued, "I set out for the Continent. I shall take up my abode in a nunnery; there I shall be quiet and unmolested." I neither expressed surprise at this resolution nor attempted to dissuade her from it. When we parted, she said: "Good-bye, cousin Jane Eyre; I wish you well." And with these words we each went our separate way.

As I shall not have occasion to refer either to her or her sister again, I may as well mention here, that Georgiana made an advantageous match with a wealthy worn-out man of fashion, and that Eliza actually took the veil, and is at this day superior of the convent where she passed the period of her novitiate, and which she endowed with her fortune.

The return to Thornfield seemed tedious – very tedious: fifty miles one day, a night spent at an inn, fifty miles the next day. I was going back to Thornfield, but how long was I to stay there? Not long, of that I was sure. I had heard from Mrs Fairfax in the interim of my absence. The party at the hall was dispersed; Mr Rochester had left for London three weeks ago, but he was then expected to return in a fortnight. Mrs Fairfax surmised that he was gone to make arrangements for his wedding, as he had talked of purchasing a new carriage. She said the idea of his marrying Miss Ingram still seemed strange to her, but from what everybody said, and from what she had herself seen, she could no longer doubt that the event would shortly take place. The question followed: 'Where was I to go?'

I had not notified to Mrs Fairfax the exact day of my return, for I did not wish a carriage to meet me at Millcote. I proposed to walk the distance quietly by myself and take the old road to Thornfield, a road which lay chiefly through fields, and was now little frequented. It was not a bright or splendid summer evening, though fair and soft. The haymakers were at work all along the road and the sky, though far from cloudless, was such as promised well for the future. I felt glad as the road shortened before me, so glad that I stopped once to ask myself what that joy meant, and to remind reason that it was not to my home I was going, or to a permanent resting-place. "Mrs Fairfax will smile you a calm welcome, to be sure," said I, "and little Adèle will clap her hands and jump to see you, but you know very well you are thinking of another than they, and that he is not thinking of you."

But what is so headstrong as youth? What so blind as inexperience? It was pleasure enough to have the privilege of again looking on Mr Rochester, whether he looked on me or not. "Hasten! hasten! Be with him while you may, but a few more days or weeks, at most, and you are parted from him for ever!" And then I strangled a new-born agony – and ran on.

They are making hay, too, in Thornfield meadows: or rather, the labourers are just quitting their work, and returning home with their rakes on their shoulders, now, at the hour I arrive. I see the narrow stile with stone steps and I see – Mr Rochester sitting there, a book and a pencil in his hand. He is writing. Well, every nerve I have is unstrung; for a moment I am beyond my own mastery. What does it mean? I did not think I should tremble in this way when I saw him, or lose my voice or the power of motion in his presence. I know another way to the house. It does not signify if I knew twenty ways, for he has seen me.

"Hello!" he cries and he puts up his book and his pencil. "There you are! Come on, if you please."

I suppose I do come on, though in what fashion I know not, being scarcely cognisant of my movements, and solicitous only to appear calm and, above all, to control the working muscles of my face and behave with decent composure.

"And this is Jane Eyre? Are you coming from Millcote, and on foot? Yes – just one of your tricks to steal into the vicinage of your home along with twilight, just as if you were a dream or a shade. What the deuce have you done with yourself this last month?"

"I have been with my aunt, sir, who is dead."

"A true Janian reply! Good angels be my guard! She comes from the other world – from the abode of people who are dead and tells me so when she meets me alone here in the gloaming! Absent from me a whole month, and forgetting me quite, I'll be sworn!"

I knew there would be pleasure in meeting my master again, even though broken by the fear that he was so soon to cease to be my master, and by the knowledge that I was nothing to him; but there was ever in Mr Rochester such a power of communicating happiness, that to taste but of the crumbs he scattered to stray and stranger birds like me, was to feast genially. I inquired soon if he had not been to London.

"Yes. And know you what I went to do?"

"Oh, yes, sir! Everybody knew your errand."

"You must see the carriage, Jane, and tell me if you don't think it will suit Mrs Rochester exactly and whether she won't look like Queen Boadicea, leaning back against those purple cushions. I wish, Jane, I were a trifle better adapted to match with her externally. Can't you give me a charm, to make me a handsome man?"

"It would be past the power of magic, sir," and, in thought I added, "A loving eye is all the charm needed; to such you are handsome enough."

Mr Rochester had sometimes read my unspoken thoughts. In the present instance he smiled at me with a certain smile; it was the real sunshine of feeling – he shed it over me now.

"Pass, Jane," said he, making room for me to cross the stile, "go up home, and stay your weary little wandering feet."

## Chapter 22

I got over the stile without a word, and meant to leave him calmly. An impulse held me fast – a force turned me round. I said – or something in me said for me, and in spite of me –

"Thank you, Mr Rochester, for your great kindness. I am strangely glad to get back again to you and wherever you are is my home – my only home."

I walked on so fast that even he could hardly have overtaken me had he tried. Little Adèle was half wild with delight when she saw me. Mrs Fairfax received me with her usual plain friendliness. There is no happiness like that of being loved by your fellow-creatures and feeling that your presence is an addition to their comfort.

A fortnight of dubious calm succeeded my return to Thornfield Hall. Nothing was said of the master's marriage, and I saw no preparation going on for such an event. One thing specially surprised me, and that was, there were no journeyings backward and forward, no visits to Ingram Park. I began to cherish hopes I had no right to conceive: that the match was broken off; that rumour had been mistaken; that one or both parties had changed their minds. Never had he called me more frequently to his presence, never been kinder to me when there – and, alas! Never had I loved him so well.

# Chapter 23

A splendid Midsummer shone over England: rare were skies so pure, suns so radiant as were then seen in long succession. The hay was all got in; the fields round Thornfield were green and shorn; the roads white and baked; the trees were in their dark prime; hedge and wood, full-leaved and deeply tinted, contrasted well with the sunny hue of the cleared meadows between.

On Midsummer-eve, Adèle, weary with gathering wild strawberries half the day, had gone to bed with the sun. I watched her drop asleep, and when I left her, I sought the garden. At the bottom was a winding walk, bordered with laurels and terminating in a giant horse-chestnut, circled at the base by a seat. Here one could wander unseen. But my step is stayed – not by sound, not by sight, but by a warning fragrance.

This new scent is neither of shrub nor flower; it is – I know it well – it is Mr Rochester's cigar. I step aside into the ivy recess. He will not stay long; he will soon return whence he came, and if I sit still he will never see me.

But no – he said quietly, without turning –

"Jane, come and look at this fellow."

I had made no noise; he had not eyes behind – could his shadow feel? I approached him.

"Look at his wings," said he, "he reminds me rather of a West Indian insect. There! He is flown." The moth roamed away.

I did not like to walk at this hour alone with Mr Rochester in the shadowy orchard, but I could not find a reason to allege for leaving him. "Jane," he recommenced as we entered the laurel walk, and slowly strayed down in

# Chapter 23

the direction the horse-chestnut. "You must have become in some degree attached to Thornfield."

"I am attached to it, indeed."

"And to that foolish little child Adèle, too, and even Dame Fairfax?"

"Yes, sir – in different ways. I have an affection for both."

"And would be sorry to part with them?"

"Yes."

"Pity!" he said, and sighed and paused. "It is always the way of events in this life," he continued presently, "no sooner have you got settled in a pleasant resting-place, than a voice calls out to you to rise and move on, for the hour of repose is expired."

"Must I move on, sir?" I asked. "Must I leave Thornfield?"

"I believe you must, Jane. I am sorry."

"Then you are going to be married, sir?"

"Ex-act-ly – pre-cise-ly; with your usual acuteness, you have hit the nail straight on the head."

"Soon, sir?"

"Very soon, and you'll remember, Jane, the first time I intimated to you that it was my intention to take Miss Ingram, and that in that case both you and little Adèle had better trot forthwith. Adèle must go to school and you, Miss Eyre, must get a new situation."

"Yes, sir, I will advertise immediately and meantime, I suppose—"

"In about a month I hope to be a bridegroom," continued Mr Rochester; "and in the interim, I shall myself look out for employment for you."

"Thank you, sir; I am sorry to give—"

"Oh, no need to apologise! Indeed I have already heard of a place that I think will suit: it is to undertake the education of the five daughters of Mrs O'Gall in Ireland. You'll like Ireland, I think. They're such warm-hearted people there, they say."

"It is a long way off, sir."

"No matter – a girl of your sense will not object to the voyage or the distance."

"Not the voyage, but the distance, and then the sea is a barrier—"

"From what, Jane?"

"From England and from Thornfield: and—"

"Well?"

"From you, sir."

And, with as little sanction of free will, my tears gushed out.

"We have been good friends, Jane, have we not?"

"Yes, sir."

"And when friends are on the eve of separation, they like to spend the little time that remains to them close to each other. Come! Here is the chestnut tree; here is the bench at its old roots. Come, we will sit there in peace to-night, though we should never more be destined to sit there together." He seated me and himself.

"I sometimes have a queer feeling with regard to you," he said, "especially when you are near me, as now. It is as if I had a string somewhere under my left ribs, tightly and inextricably knotted to a similar string situated in the corresponding quarter of your little frame. And if that boisterous Channel, and two hundred miles or so of land come broad between us, I am afraid that cord of communion will be snapped, and then I've a nervous notion I should take to bleeding inwardly. As for you – you'd forget me."

"That I never should, sir. You know—" I sobbed convulsively, for I could repress what I endured no longer; I was obliged to yield, and I was shaken from head to foot with acute distress. When I did speak, it was only to express an impetuous wish that I had never been born, or never come to Thornfield.

"I grieve to leave Thornfield. I love Thornfield – I love it, because I have lived in it a full and delightful life – I have not been trampled on. I have

## Chapter 23

not been petrified. I have known you, Mr Rochester, and it strikes me with terror and anguish to feel I absolutely must be torn from you for ever. I see the necessity of departure and it is like looking on the necessity of death."

"Where do you see the necessity?" he asked suddenly.

"Where? You, sir, have placed it before me."

"In what shape?"

"In the shape of Miss Ingram: a noble and beautiful woman – your bride."

"My bride! What bride? I have no bride!"

"But you will have."

"Yes – I will! – I will!" He set his teeth.

"Then I must go – you have said it yourself."

"No! You must stay! I swear it – and the oath shall be kept."

"I tell you I must go!" I retorted, roused to something like passion. "Do you think I can stay to become nothing to you? Do you think I am an automaton? A machine without feelings? Do you think, because I am poor, obscure, plain, and little, I am soulless and heartless? You think wrong! I have as much soul as you – and full as much heart! And if God had gifted me with some beauty and much wealth, I should have made it as hard for you to leave me, as it is now for me to leave you. It is my spirit that addresses your spirit; as if both we stood at God's feet, equal – as we are!"

"As we are!" repeated Mr Rochester; "so," he added, enclosing me in his arms, gathering me to his breast, pressing his lips on my lips, "so, Jane!"

"Yes, so, sir," I rejoined, "and yet not so; for you are a married man – or as good as a married man – let me go!"

"Jane, be still; don't struggle so, like a wild frantic bird."

"I am no bird, and no net ensnares me. I am a free human being with an independent will, which I now exert to leave you."

Another effort set me at liberty, and I stood erect before him.

"And your will shall decide your destiny," he said. "I offer you my hand, my heart, and a share of all my possessions. I ask you to pass through life at my side – to be my second self, and best earthly companion."

"You have already made your choice and must abide by it."

"Jane, be still a few moments: it is you only I intend to marry."

I was silent; I thought he mocked me.

"Come, Jane – come hither."

"Your bride stands between us."

He rose, and with a stride reached me. "My bride is here," he said, again drawing me to him, "because my equal is here, and my likeness. Jane, will you marry me?"

Still I did not answer, and still I writhed myself from his grasp, for I was still incredulous.

"Do you doubt me, Jane?"

"Entirely."

"You have no faith in me?"

"Not a whit."

"Am I a liar in your eyes?" he asked passionately. "I would not – I could not – marry Miss Ingram. You – you almost unearthly thing – I love as my own flesh. You – poor and obscure, and small and plain as you are – I entreat to accept me as a husband."

"What, me!" I exclaimed, beginning to credit his sincerity, "me who have not a friend in the world but you?"

"You, Jane, I must have you for my own – entirely my own. Will you be mine? Say yes, quickly."

"Are you in earnest? Do you truly love me? Do you sincerely wish me to be your wife?"

"I do and if an oath is necessary to satisfy you, I swear it."

"Then, sir, I will marry you."

# Chapter 23

"Come to me – come to me entirely now," said he, and added, in his deepest tone, speaking in my ear as his cheek was laid on mine, "Make my happiness – I will make yours."

"God pardon me!" he subjoined ere long, "and man meddle not with me; I have her, and will hold her."

"There is no one to meddle, sir. I have no kindred to interfere."

"No – that is the best of it," he said.

But what had befallen the night? The moon was not yet set, and we were all in shadow. I could scarcely see my master's face, near as I was. And what ailed the chestnut tree? it writhed and groaned, while wind roared in the laurel walk and came sweeping over us.

"We must go in," said Mr Rochester, "the weather changes."

Just then a livid, vivid spark leapt out of a cloud at which I was looking, and there was a crack, a crash, and a close rattling peal, and I thought only of hiding my dazzled eyes against Mr Rochester's shoulder. The rain rushed down. He hurried me up the walk, through the grounds, and into the house, but we were quite wet before we could pass the threshold. He was taking off my shawl in the hall, and shaking the water out of my loosened hair, when Mrs Fairfax emerged from her room. I did not observe her at first, nor did Mr Rochester. The lamp was lit. The clock was on the stroke of twelve.

"Good-night, my darling!"

He kissed me repeatedly. When I looked up, on leaving his arms, there stood Mrs Fairfax, pale, grave, and amazed. I only smiled at her and ran upstairs. "Explanation will do for another time," thought I.

When I reached my chamber, joy effaced every other feeling; and loud as the wind blew, near and deep as the thunder crashed, fierce and frequent as the lightning gleamed, cataract-like as the rain fell during a storm of two hours' duration, I experienced no fear and little awe.

Before I left my bed in the morning, little Adèle came running in to tell me that the great horse-chestnut at the bottom of the orchard had been struck by lightning in the night, and half of it split away.

# Chapter 24

As I rose and dressed, I thought over what had happened, and wondered if it were a dream.

While arranging my hair, I looked at my face in the glass, and felt it was no longer plain. There was hope in its aspect and life in its colour. I had often been unwilling to look at my master because I feared he could not be pleased at my look, but I was sure I might lift my face to his now. I took a plain but clean and light summer dress from my drawer and put it on. It seemed no attire had ever so well become me, because none had I ever worn in so blissful a mood.

I was not surprised, when I ran down into the hall, to see that a brilliant June morning had succeeded to the tempest of the night, and to feel, through the open glass door, the breathing of a fresh and fragrant breeze. Nature must be gladsome when I was so happy. The rooks cawed, and blither birds sang, but nothing was so merry or so musical as my own rejoicing heart.

Mrs Fairfax surprised me by looking with a sad countenance, and saying gravely, "Miss Eyre, will you come to breakfast?" During the meal she was quiet and cool. I must wait for my master to give explanations and so must she. I ate what I could, and then I hastened upstairs. I met Adèle leaving the schoolroom.

"Where are you going? It is time for lessons."

"Mr Rochester has sent me away to the nursery."

"Where is he?"

"In there," pointing to the apartment she had left. I went in, and there he stood.

# Chapter 24

"Come and bid me good-morning," said he. I gladly advanced and received an embrace and a kiss. It seemed natural; it seemed genial to be so well loved, so caressed by him.

"Jane, you look blooming, and smiling, and pretty," said he, "truly pretty this morning. Soon to be Jane Rochester," he added, "in four weeks, Jane, not a day more. Do you hear that?"

I did, and I could not quite comprehend it.

"Yes, Mrs Rochester," said he.

"It can never be, sir. It does not sound likely. To imagine such a lot befalling me is a fairy tale – a day-dream."

"Which I can and will realise. This morning I wrote to my banker in London to send me certain jewels he has in his keeping – heirlooms for the ladies of Thornfield. In a day or two I hope to pour them into your lap; for every privilege, every attention shall be yours that I would accord a peer's daughter, if about to marry her."

"Oh, sir! Never rain jewels! Jewels for Jane Eyre sounds unnatural and strange. I would rather not have them."

"I will myself put the diamond chain round your neck, and the circlet on your forehead, Jane, and I will clasp the bracelets on these fine wrists and load these fingers with rings."

"No, no, sir! Speak of other things, and in another strain. Don't address me as if I were a beauty; I am your plain governess."

He went on, "I will attire my Jane in satin and lace, and she shall have roses in her hair, and I will cover the head I love best with a priceless veil."

"And then you won't know me, sir, and I shall not be your Jane Eyre any longer, but an ape in a harlequin's jacket – I don't call you handsome, sir, though I love you most dearly. Don't flatter me."

He pursued his theme, however. "This very day I shall take you in the carriage to Millcote and you must choose some dresses for yourself. I told you we shall be married in four weeks. The wedding is to take place quietly and then I shall waft you away at once to town. After a brief stay there, I shall bear my treasure to regions nearer the sun, to French vineyards and Italian plains."

"Shall I travel? And with you, sir?"

"You shall sojourn at Paris, Rome, and Naples; at Florence, Venice, and Vienna; all the ground I have wandered over shall be re-trodden by you. Now I shall revisit it healed and cleansed, with a very angel as my comforter. Ask me something, Jane – the least thing. I desire to be entreated—"

"Well then, sir, gratify my curiosity, which is much piqued on one point."

He looked disturbed. "What? What?" he said hastily. "Curiosity is a dangerous petition."

"How stern you look now! That will be your married look, sir, I suppose?"

"But what had you to ask, out with it?"

"This is what I have to ask – why did you take such pains to make me believe you wished to marry Miss Ingram?"

"Is that all? Thank God it is no worse!" And now he unknit his black brows and looked down, smiling at me.

"Well, I feigned courtship of Miss Ingram, because I wished to render you as madly in love with me as I was with you, and I knew jealousy would be the best ally I could call in for the furtherance of that end."

"Did you think nothing of Miss Ingram's feelings, sir?"

"Her feelings are concentrated in one – pride. Were you jealous, Jane?"

"Won't she feel forsaken and deserted?"

"Impossible! When I told you how she, on the contrary, deserted me: the idea of my lack of wealth cooled, or rather extinguished, her flame in a moment."

I turned my lips to the hand that lay on my shoulder. I loved him very much – more than I could trust myself to say – more than words had power to express.

"Ask something more," he said presently.

# Chapter 24

I was again ready with my request. "Communicate your intentions to Mrs Fairfax, sir. She saw me with you last night in the hall, and she was shocked. Give her some explanation before I see her again. It pains me to be misjudged by so good a woman. I believe she thought I had forgotten my station, and yours, sir."

A while later, when I heard Mr Rochester quit Mrs Fairfax's parlour, I hurried down to it. Seeing me, she roused herself, made a sort of effort to smile, and framed a few words of congratulation, but the smile expired, and the sentence was abandoned unfinished.

"I feel so astonished," she began, "I hardly know what to say to you, Miss Eyre. It is actually true that Mr Rochester has asked you to marry him? He came in here five minutes ago and said that in a month you would be his wife."

"He has said the same thing to me," I replied.

"He has! Do you believe him? Have you accepted him?"

"Yes."

She looked at me bewildered.

"I could never have thought it. He means to marry you?"

"He tells me so."

She surveyed my whole person. In her eyes I read that they had there found no charm powerful enough to solve the enigma.

"How it will answer," she continued, "I cannot tell; I really don't know. Equality of position and fortune is often advisable in such cases, and there are twenty years of difference in your ages. He might almost be your father."

"No, indeed, Mrs Fairfax!" exclaimed I, nettled.

"Is it really for love he is going to marry you?" she asked.

I was so hurt by her coldness and scepticism, that the tears rose to my eyes.

"Why? Am I a monster?" I said. "Is it impossible that Mr Rochester should have a sincere affection for me?"

"No, you are very well, but I have been a little uneasy at his marked preference and have wished to put you on your guard. Last night I cannot tell you what I suffered when I could find you nowhere, nor the master either, and then, at twelve o'clock, saw you come in with him. I hope all will be right in the end, but believe me, you cannot be too careful. Try and keep Mr Rochester at a distance. Gentlemen in his station are not accustomed to marry their governesses."

Just then the message came that the carriage was ready to take us to Millcote; they were bringing it round to the front.

The hour spent at Millcote was a somewhat harassing one to me. Mr Rochester obliged me to go to a silk warehouse. There I was ordered to choose half-a-dozen dresses. I hated the business; I begged leave to defer it. I watched his eye rove over the gay stores. He fixed on a rich silk of the most brilliant amethyst dye, and a superb pink satin. With infinite difficulty, for he was stubborn as a stone, I persuaded him to make an exchange in favour of a sober black satin and pearl-grey silk. "It might pass for the present," he said, "but he would yet see me glittering."

Glad was I to get him out of the silk warehouse, and then out of a jeweller's shop. The more he bought me, the more my cheek burned with a sense of annoyance and degradation. I remembered the letter of my uncle, John Eyre, to Mrs Reed, and his intention to adopt me and make me his legatee. "It would, indeed, be a relief," I thought, "if I had ever so small an independency; I never can bear being dressed like a doll by Mr Rochester. I will write to Madeira the moment I get home, and tell my uncle John I am going to be married, and to whom. And somewhat relieved by this idea I ventured once more to meet my lover's eye, and I thought his smile was such as a sultan might, in a blissful and fond moment, bestow on a slave his gold and gems had enriched. I crushed his hand, which was ever hunting mine, and thrust it back to him red with the passionate pressure.

We were now approaching Thornfield. "Will it please you to dine with me to-day?" he asked, as we re-entered the gates.

## Chapter 24

"No, thank you, sir. I never have dined with you, sir, and I see no reason why I should now."

"You will give up your governessing at once."

"Indeed, begging your pardon, sir, I shall not. I shall just go on with it as usual. I shall keep out of your way all day, as I have been accustomed to do. You may send for me in the evening when you feel disposed to see me, and I'll come then, but at no other time."

He continued to send for me punctually the moment the clock struck seven, and when the hour came to retire I got up, and saying, "I wish you good-night, sir," in my natural and wonted respectful manner, I slipped out by the side-door and got away. The system thus entered on, I pursued during the whole season of probation and with the best success. Mrs Fairfax, I saw, approved me, and her anxiety on my account vanished.

Yet, after all, my task was not an easy one; often I would rather have pleased than teased him. My future husband was becoming to me my whole world and more than the world, almost my hope of heaven. He stood between me and every thought of religion, as an eclipse intervenes between man and the broad sun. I could not, in those days, see God for His creature: of whom I had made an idol.

# Chapter 25

There was no putting off the day that advanced – the bridal day and all preparations for its arrival were complete. I, at least, had nothing more to do. There were my trunks, packed, locked, corded, ranged in a row along the wall of my little chamber. To-morrow, at this time, they would be far on their road to London and so should I, or rather, not I, but one Jane Rochester. Mrs Rochester! She did not exist. She would not be born till to-morrow, some time after eight o'clock a.m. It was enough that in yonder closet, opposite my dressing-table, garments said to be hers had already displaced my black Lowood frock and straw bonnet: a suit of wedding raiment; the pearl-coloured robe, the vapoury veil hanging from the cupboard. I shut the closet to conceal the strange apparel, which, at this evening hour, gave out a ghostly shimmer. "I am feverish," I said, "I hear the wind blowing; I will go out of doors and feel it."

It was not only the hurry of preparation that made me feverish, not only the anticipation of the great change – the new life which was to commence to-morrow – but a third cause influenced my mind more than they.

I had at heart a strange and anxious thought. Something had taken place the preceding night. Mr Rochester was absent from home; I waited now his return, eager to unburden my mind and to seek of him the solution of the enigma that perplexed me.

I sought the orchard, driven to its shelter by the wind, which all day had blown strong and full, without, however, bringing a speck of rain. Descending the laurel walk, I faced the wreck of the chestnut-tree; it stood up black and riven, the trunk split down the centre. The cloven halves were not broken from each other, for the firm base and strong roots kept them unsundered below. Their great boughs on each side were dead, and next winter's tempests would be sure to fell one or both to earth. As yet, however, they might be said to form one tree.

"I wish he would come! I wish he would come!" I exclaimed. I had expected his arrival before tea; now it was dark: what could keep him? The event of last night again recurred to me. I interpreted it as a warning of disaster. I had enjoyed so much bliss lately that I imagined my fortune must now decline.

Just then I heard the tramp of hoofs. It was he. I now ran to meet him.

"There!" he exclaimed, as he stretched out his hand and bent from the saddle. "You can't do without me, that is evident. Step on my boot-toe; give me both hands: mount!"

I obeyed; joy made me agile. I sprang up before him.

"But is there anything the matter, Jane, that you come to meet me at such an hour? Is there anything wrong?"

"No, but I thought you would never come. I could not bear to wait in the house for you, especially with this rain and wind."

"Rain and wind, indeed!"

Shortly, we reached Thornfield and he let me get down. Having followed me into the hall, he told me to make haste and put something dry on and then return to him in the library, where I rejoined him and found him at supper.

"Bear me company, Jane. It is the last meal but one you will eat at Thornfield Hall for a long time."

I sat down near him but told him I could not eat.

"Are you well?"

"I believe I am."

"Believe! What is the matter? Tell me what you feel. You have been over-excited, or over-fatigued."

I looked up at him to read the signs of bliss in his face; it was ardent and flushed.

"What do you fear, Jane?" he said. "Are you apprehensive of the new sphere you are about to enter? Of the new life into which you are passing?"

"No."

"Jane, I want an explanation."

"Then, sir, listen. All day yesterday I was very busy, and very happy. I walked a little while after tea, thinking of you, and just at sunset, as the air turned cold and the sky cloudy, I went in and then upstairs to look at my wedding-dress, which they had just brought, and under it in the box I found your present – the veil which, in your princely extravagance, you sent for from London.

"Some time after I went to bed, but I could not sleep – a sense of anxious excitement distressed me. The gale still rising seemed to my ear a mournful sound, which at last I made out must be some dog howling at a distance. On sleeping, I continued in dreams the idea of a dark and gusty night. I was following the windings of an unknown road; rain pelted me. I was burdened with the charge of a little child: a very small creature, too young and feeble to walk, and which shivered in my cold arms, and wailed piteously. You were on the road a long way before me and I strained every nerve to overtake you, and made effort on effort to utter your name and entreat you to stop – but my movements were fettered and my voice died away while you withdrew farther and farther every moment."

"And these dreams weigh on your spirits now, Jane, when I am close to you? Forget visionary woe and think only of real happiness! Do you love me, Jane? Repeat it."

"I do, sir – I do, with my whole heart, but hear me to the end."

"What! Is there more? Go on."

"I dreamt another dream, sir: that Thornfield Hall was a dreary ruin, the retreat of bats and owls. Nothing remained but a shell-like wall, very high and very fragile-looking. I wandered through the grass-grown enclosure within. Here I stumbled over a marble hearth and there over a fallen fragment of cornice. Wrapped up in a shawl, I still carried the unknown little child. I might not lay it down anywhere, however tired were my

## Chapter 25

arms. I heard the gallop of a horse; I was sure it was you departing for many years and for a distant country. I climbed the thin wall with frantic perilous haste, eager to catch one glimpse of you from the top. I saw you like a speck on a white track, lessening every moment. The blast blew so strong the wall crumbled, the child rolled from my knee, I lost my balance, fell, and woke."

"Now, Jane, that is all."

"All the preface, sir. The tale is yet to come. On waking, a gleam dazzled my eyes. There was a light on the dressing-table, and the door of the closet, where, before going to bed, I had hung my wedding-dress and veil, stood open. I heard a rustling there. I asked, 'What are you doing?' No one answered but a form emerged. It took the light, held it aloft, and surveyed the garments hanging from the cupboard. 'Who is there?' I cried, and still it was silent. I had risen up; first surprise came over me, and then my blood crept cold through my veins. Mr Rochester, this was not any of the servants; it was not Mrs Fairfax – it was not even that strange woman, Grace Poole."

"It must have been one of them," interrupted my master.

"No, sir, I solemnly assure you to the contrary. The shape standing before me had never crossed my eyes within Thornfield Hall before."

"Describe it, Jane."

"It seemed, sir, a woman, tall and large, with thick and dark hair hanging long down her back. I know not what dress she had on; it was white and straight, but whether gown, sheet, or shroud, I cannot tell."

"Did you see her face?"

"Not at first. But presently she took my veil from its place; she held it up, gazed at it long, and then she threw it over her own head, and turned to the mirror. At that moment I saw the reflection of the visage and features quite distinctly in the dark oblong glass."

"And how were they?"

"Fearful and ghastly to me – oh, sir, I never saw a face like it! It was a discoloured face – it was a savage face. I wish I could forget the roll of the red eyes and the fearful blackened inflation of the lineaments!"

"Ghosts are usually pale, Jane."

"This, sir, was purple. The lips were swelled and dark; the brow furrowed; the black eyebrows widely raised over the bloodshot eyes. Shall I tell you of what it reminded me?"

"You may."

"Of the foul German spectre – the Vampyre."

"Ah! – what did it do?"

"Sir, it removed my veil from its gaunt head, rent it in two parts, and flinging both on the floor, trampled on them."

"Afterwards?"

"It drew aside the window-curtain and looked out; taking the candle, it retreated to the door. Just at my bedside, the figure stopped. The fiery eyes glared upon me – she thrust up her candle close to my face and extinguished it under my eyes. I was aware her lurid visage flamed over mine, and I lost consciousness, insensible from terror. Now, sir, tell me who and what that woman was?"

"The creature of an over-stimulated brain, that is certain."

"Sir, the thing was real; the transaction actually took place. When in full daylight I looked round the room, there – on the carpet – I saw the veil, torn from top to bottom in two halves!"

I felt Mr Rochester start and shudder. "Thank God!" he exclaimed, "that if anything malignant did come near you last night, it was only the veil that was harmed. Oh, to think what might have happened!"

After some minutes' silence, he continued, cheerily –

"Now, Jane, I'll explain to you all about it. It was half dream, half reality. A woman did, I doubt not, enter your room, and that woman was – must have been – Grace Poole. In a state between sleeping and waking, you noticed her entrance and her actions, but feverish, almost delirious as you were, you ascribed to her an appearance different from her own. The spiteful tearing of the veil was real. I see you would ask why I keep such a woman in my house: when we have been married a year and a day, I will tell you; but not now."

I reflected, and in truth it appeared to me the only possible solution; satisfied I was not, but to please him I answered him with a contented smile.

"The incident you have related should make you nervous, and I would rather you did not sleep alone. Promise me to go to the nursery."

"I shall be very glad to do so, sir."

"And fasten the door securely on the inside. You will not dream of separation and sorrow to-night, but of happy love and blissful union."

# Chapter 26

Sophie came at seven to dress me. She was very long in her task, so long that Mr Rochester, grown impatient, sent up to ask why I did not come. I hurried from under her hands as soon as I could.

"Stop!" she cried. "Look at yourself in the mirror; you have not taken one peep."

So I turned. I saw a robed and veiled figure, so unlike my usual self that it seemed almost the image of a stranger. "Jane!" called a voice, and I hastened down. I was received at the foot of the stairs by Mr Rochester.

"Lingerer!" he said. "My brain is on fire with impatience!"

He took me into the dining-room, surveyed me keenly all over, pronounced me "fair as a lily," then told me he would give me but ten minutes to eat some breakfast.

There were no groomsmen, no bridesmaids, no relatives; none but Mr Rochester and I. Mrs Fairfax stood in the hall as we passed. I would fain have spoken to her, but my hand was held by a grasp of iron. I was hurried along by a stride I could hardly follow. I wonder what other bridegroom ever looked as he did – so grimly resolute.

We entered the quiet and humble temple; the priest waited with the clerk beside him. All was still; two shadows only moved in a remote corner. Two strangers had slipped in before us, and they now stood by the vault of the Rochesters, their backs towards us. The service began. The priest came a step further forward and bent slightly towards Mr Rochester.

"I require and charge you both that if either of you know any impediment why ye may not lawfully be joined together in matrimony, ye do now confess it."

## Chapter 26

He paused, as the custom is. When is the pause after that sentence ever broken by reply? Not, perhaps, once in a hundred years. And the priest, who had held his breath but for a moment, was proceeding when a distinct voice said –

"The marriage cannot go on."

The priest looked up at the speaker and stood mute. Mr Rochester moved slightly and, not turning his head or eyes, he said, "Proceed."

Profound silence fell when he had uttered that word. Presently the priest said, "I cannot proceed without some investigation."

"The ceremony is quite broken off," subjoined the voice behind us. "An overwhelming impediment to this marriage exists."

Mr Rochester heard, but stood stubborn and rigid, making no movement but to possess himself of my hand. What a strong grasp he had!

The priest seemed at a loss. "What is the nature of the impediment?" he asked.

The speaker came forward, uttering each word distinctly, calmly, steadily –

"Mr Rochester has a wife now living."

I looked at Mr Rochester. His whole face was colourless rock. Without speaking, without smiling, he only twined my waist with his arm and riveted me to his side.

"Who are you?" he asked of the intruder.

"My name is Briggs, a solicitor from London."

Mr Briggs calmly took a paper from his pocket, and read out in a sort of official voice.

"'I affirm and can prove that Edward Fairfax Rochester, of Thornfield Hall, England, was married to my sister, Bertha Antoinetta Mason, in Spanish Town, Jamaica. Signed, Richard Mason.'"

"That does not prove that the woman mentioned is still living."

"She was living three months ago," returned the lawyer.

"How do you know?"

"I have a witness to the fact."

"Produce him – or go to hell."

"Mr Mason, have the goodness to step forward."

The second stranger, who had hitherto lingered in the background, now drew near. It was Mason himself. Contempt fell cool on Mr Rochester; he only asked, "What have you to say?"

"She is now living at Thornfield Hall," said Mason. "I saw her there last April. I am her brother."

"At Thornfield Hall!" exclaimed the priest. "Impossible! I am an old resident in this neighbourhood, sir, and I never heard of a Mrs Rochester at Thornfield Hall."

I saw a grim smile contort Mr Rochester's lips, and he muttered –

"No, by God! I took care that none should hear of it – or of her under that name." He paused. "Enough! Close your book. There will be no wedding to-day." The man obeyed.

Mr Rochester continued recklessly: "Gentlemen, what this lawyer and his client say is true. I have been married, and the woman to whom I was married lives! You say you never heard of a Mrs Rochester at the house, but I daresay you have many a time inclined your ear to gossip about the mysterious lunatic kept there under watch. I now inform you that she is my wife, whom I married fifteen years ago – Bertha Mason by name. She is mad and she came of a mad family; idiots and maniacs through three generations – as I found out after I had wed. I invite you all to come up to the house and visit Mrs Poole's patient, and my wife! You shall see what sort of a being I was cheated into espousing, and judge whether or not I had a right to break my vows. This girl," he continued, looking at me, "knew no more than you of the disgusting secret. She thought all was fair and legal. Come all of you – follow!"

Still holding me fast, he left the church; the three gentlemen came after.

At our entrance, Mrs Fairfax, Adèle, Sophie and Leah advanced to meet and greet us.

# Chapter 26

"Away with your congratulations!" cried the master.

He passed on and ascended the stairs, still holding my hand. We mounted the first staircase and proceeded to the third storey. The low, black door, opened by Mr Rochester's master-key, admitted us to the tapestried room.

"You know this place, Mason," said our guide, "she bit and stabbed you here."

He lifted the hangings from the wall, uncovering the second door. This, too, he opened. In a room without a window, there burnt a fire, and a lamp was suspended from the ceiling by a chain. Grace Poole bent over the fire, apparently cooking something in a saucepan. In the deep shade, at the farther end of the room, a figure ran backwards and forwards. What it was, whether beast or human being, one could not, at first sight, tell. It grovelled, seemingly, on all fours; it snatched and growled like some strange wild animal, but it was covered with clothing, and a quantity of dark, grizzled hair, wild as a mane, hid its head and face.

"Good-morrow, Mrs Poole!" said Mr Rochester. "How are you? And how is your charge to-day?"

"We're tolerable, sir, I thank you," replied Grace.

A fierce cry seemed to give the lie to her favourable report. The clothed hyena rose up and stood tall on its hind-feet.

"Take care, sir! For God's sake, take care!"

The maniac bellowed. She parted her shaggy locks and gazed wildly at her visitors. I recognised well that purple face, those bloated features. Mrs Poole advanced.

"Keep out of the way," said Mr Rochester, thrusting her aside, "she has no knife now, I suppose, and I'm on my guard."

"One never knows what she has, sir. She is so cunning."

"We had better leave her," whispered Mason.

"Go to the devil!" was his brother-in-law's recommendation.

"Beware!" cried Grace. The three gentlemen retreated simultaneously. Mr Rochester flung me behind him. The lunatic sprang and grappled his throat viciously and laid her teeth to his cheek. They struggled. She was a big woman, in stature almost equalling her husband, and corpulent besides. She showed virile force in the contest – more than once she almost throttled him, athletic as he was. At last, he mastered her arms; Grace Poole gave him a cord, and he bound her to a chair. The operation was performed amidst the fiercest yells and the most convulsive plunges. Mr Rochester then turned to the spectators with a smile both bitter and desolate.

"That is my wife," said he. "Such is the sole embrace I am ever to know! And this is what I wished to have," (laying his hand on my shoulder) "this young girl, who stands so quiet at the mouth of hell, looking collectedly at a demon. Look at the difference then judge me, priest of the gospel and man of the law! Off with you now. I must shut up my prize."

We all withdrew. Mr Rochester stayed a moment behind us, to give some further order to Grace Poole. The solicitor addressed me as he descended the stair.

"You, madam," said he, "are cleared from all blame: your uncle will be glad to hear it – if, indeed, he should be still living – when Mr Mason returns to Madeira."

"My uncle! What of him? Do you know him?"

"Mr Mason does. Mr Eyre has been a correspondent for some years. When your uncle received your letter intimating the contemplated union between yourself and Mr Rochester, Mr Mason revealed the real state of matters. Your uncle, I am sorry to say, is now on a sick bed and it is unlikely he will ever rise. He could not then hasten to England himself, to extricate you from the snare into which you had fallen, but he implored Mr Mason to lose no time in taking steps to prevent the false marriage."

"Come– let us be gone," said Mr Mason, anxiously, and without waiting to take leave of Mr Rochester, they made their exit. The house cleared, I shut myself in, fastened the bolt that none might intrude, and proceeded – not to weep, I was yet too calm for that – but mechanically to take off the wedding dress, and replace it by the gown I had worn yesterday. I

## Chapter 26

then sat down. I felt weak and tired. I leaned my arms on a table, and my head dropped on them. The transaction in the church had not been noisy; there was no explosion of passion, no loud dispute; an open admission of the truth had been uttered by my master; then the living proof had been seen and all was over.

I was in my own room as usual – just myself, without obvious change. And yet where was the Jane Eyre of yesterday? Where was her life? Where were her prospects? Jane Eyre, who had been an ardent, expectant woman – almost a bride, was a cold, solitary girl again. Her life was pale; her prospects were desolate. A Christmas frost had come at midsummer; a white December storm had whirled over June. My hopes were all dead – struck with a subtle doom. I looked on my cherished wishes. They lay chill. I looked at my love; it shivered in my heart, like a suffering child in a cold cradle. Oh, never more could it turn to Mr Rochester, for faith was destroyed! Mr Rochester was not to me what he had been, for he was not what I had thought him. I would not say he had betrayed me but from his presence I must go – that I perceived well. When – how – whither, I could not yet discern. Real affection, it seemed, he could not have for me; he would want me no more. I should fear even to cross his path now. My view must be hateful to him. Oh, how blind had been my eyes! How weak my conduct!

My eyes were covered and closed. Darkness seemed to swim round me. I lay faint, longing to be dead. One idea only still throbbed life-like within me – a remembrance of God and an unuttered prayer:

"Be not far from me, for trouble is near: there is none to help."

It was near and I had neither joined my hands, nor moved my lips in prayer. It came, the whole consciousness of my lonely life; my love lost, my hope quenched, poured over me. That bitter hour cannot be described. In truth, "the waters came into my soul; I came into deep waters; the floods overflowed me."

# Chapter 27

Some time in the afternoon I raised my head and asked, "What am I to do?"

But the answer my mind gave – "Leave Thornfield at once" – was so prompt, so dread, that I stopped my ears. I could not bear such words now. "That I must leave him decidedly, instantly, is intolerable. I cannot do it." I wrestled with my own resolution. I wanted to be weak that I might avoid the awful suffering I saw laid out for me.

I rose up and my head swam as I stood. Neither meat nor drink had passed my lips that day, for I had taken no breakfast. As I undrew the bolt and stepped out, I stumbled over an obstacle. I fell, but not on to the ground. An outstretched arm caught me. I looked up – I was supported by Mr Rochester, who sat in a chair across my chamber threshold.

"You come out at last," he said. "Well, I have been waiting for you long, and listening, yet not one movement have I heard, nor one sob. Five minutes more of that death-like hush, and I should have forced the lock like a burglar. So you shun me? You shut yourself up and grieve alone! You are passionate; I expected a scene of some kind. But you have not wept at all! I see no trace of tears.

"Well, Jane! not a word of reproach? Nothing bitter? I never meant to wound you thus. Will you ever forgive me?"

Reader, I forgave him at the moment. There was such deep remorse in his eye, and besides, there was such unchanged love in his whole look – I forgave him all, yet not in words, only at my heart's core.

"You know I am a scoundrel, Jane?"

"Yes, sir."

## Chapter 27

"Then tell me so – don't spare me."

"I cannot. I am tired and sick. I want some water." He heaved a sort of shuddering sigh, and taking me in his arms, carried me downstairs. Presently I felt the reviving warmth of a fire, for, summer as it was, I had become icy cold in my chamber. He put wine to my lips; I tasted it and revived. Then I ate something he offered me and was soon myself. I was in the library – sitting in his chair – he was quite near.

"How are you now, Jane?"

"Much better, sir; I shall be well soon."

Suddenly he stooped towards me as if to kiss me, but I remembered caresses were now forbidden. I turned my face away.

"What! How is this?" he exclaimed. "Oh, you won't kiss the husband of Bertha Mason? You consider me a married man. You intend to make yourself a complete stranger to me, to live under this roof only as Adèle's governess. If ever I say a friendly word to you, you will say: 'That man had nearly made me his mistress. I must be ice and rock to him.' And ice and rock you will become."

I cleared and steadied my voice to reply. "All is changed about me, sir; I must change too – there is only one way – Adèle must have a new governess, sir."

"Oh, Adèle will go to school – I have settled that already. Nor do I mean to torment you with the hideous associations and recollections of Thornfield Hall. Jane, you shall not stay here, nor will I. I'll shut up Thornfield Hall. I'll give Mrs Poole two hundred a year to live here with my wife. Grace will do much for money, and when my wife is prompted to burn people in their beds at night, to stab them and so on—"

"Sir," I interrupted him, "you are cruel – she cannot help being mad."

"Jane, my darling, it is not because she is mad I hate her. If you were mad, do you think I should hate you?"

"I do indeed, sir."

"Then you are mistaken. Every atom of your flesh is as dear to me as my own. Even if you flew at me as wildly as that woman did this morning, I should not shrink from you with disgust as I did from her. But why do I follow that train of ideas? I was talking of removing you from Thornfield. I have a place to repair to, which will be a sanctuary even from falsehood and slander."

"And take Adèle with you, sir," I interrupted; "she will be a companion for you. Retirement and solitude are too dull for you."

"Solitude! Solitude!" he reiterated with irritation. "You are to share my solitude!"

I shook my head. He had been walking fast about the room, and he stopped, as if suddenly rooted to one spot. He looked at me long and hard. I turned my eyes from him, fixed them on the fire, and tried to assume and maintain a quiet, collected aspect.

"Jane! Will you hear reason?"

"Sit down. I'll talk to you as long as you like, and hear all you have to say, whether reasonable or unreasonable."

He sat down but he did not get leave to speak directly. I had been struggling with tears for some time; I had taken great pains to repress them. Now, however, I considered it well to let them flow. If the flood annoyed him, so much the better. So I gave way and cried heartily.

Soon I heard him entreating me to be composed. I said I could not while he was in such a passion.

"But I am not angry, Jane. I only love you too well, and you had steeled your little pale face with such a resolute, frozen look – I could not endure it. Hush, now, and wipe your eyes."

Now he made an effort to draw me to him: no.

"Jane! Jane!" he said, "you don't love me, then? It was only the rank of my wife that you valued?"

These words cut me.

"I do love you," I said, "more than ever, and this is the last time I must express it."

## Chapter 27

"The last time, Jane! What! Do you think you can live with me, and see me daily, and yet, if you still love me, be always cold and distant?"

"No, sir; that I am certain I could not and therefore I see there is but one way: I must leave you."

"For how long, Jane?"

"I must part with you for my whole life. I must begin a new existence among strange faces and strange scenes."

"Of course. We shall go to a place I have in the south of France; a villa on the shores of the Mediterranean. There you shall live a happy and most innocent life. I am not married. You shall be Mrs Rochester. Why did you shake your head? Jane, you must be reasonable."

His voice and hand quivered. Still I dared to speak.

"Sir, your wife is living; that is a fact acknowledged this morning by yourself. If I lived with you as you desire, I should then be your mistress."

"I am a fool!" cried Mr Rochester suddenly. "I keep telling her I am not married, and do not explain to her why. I will in a few words show you the real state of the case. Can you listen to me?"

"Yes, sir."

"Jane, did you ever hear or know that I had once a brother older than I?"

"I remember Mrs Fairfax told me so once."

"My father was an avaricious man and it was his resolution to keep the property together. He could not bear the idea of dividing his estate and leaving me a fair portion. All, he resolved, should go to my brother, Rowland. Yet I must be provided for by a wealthy marriage. Mr Mason, a West India merchant, was his old acquaintance. Mr Mason had a daughter who would inherit a fortune of thirty thousand pounds. When I left college, I was sent out to Jamaica. My father said nothing about her money but he told me Miss Mason was the boast of Spanish Town for her beauty, and this was no lie. They showed her to me in parties. I seldom saw her alone and had very little private conversation with her. All the men in her circle seemed to admire her and envy me. I was dazzled, and being ignorant and inexperienced, I thought I loved her. A marriage was achieved almost before I knew where I was. Oh, I have no respect for myself when I think of that act! I never loved, and I did not even know her.

"My bride's mother I had never seen; I understood she was dead. The honeymoon over, I learned my mistake; she was only mad, and shut up in a lunatic asylum. There was a younger brother, too – a complete idiot. My father and my brother Rowland knew all this, but they thought only of the thirty thousand pounds.

"These were vile discoveries; but I should have made them no subject of reproach to my wife, even when I found her nature wholly alien to mine, her mind low and incapable of being led to anything higher – when I found that I could not pass a single hour of the day with her in comfort, that kindly conversation could not be sustained between us – when I perceived that I should never have a quiet household, because no servant would bear the continued outbreaks of her violent temper or her absurd orders. Even then I restrained myself. I tried to devour my disgust in secret.

"Jane, I will not trouble you with abominable details. I lived with that woman upstairs four years. Her character developed with frightful rapidity; her vices sprang up fast and rank. They were so strong, only cruelty could check them, and I would not use cruelty. Bertha Mason dragged me through all the degrading agonies which must attend a man bound to a wife at once intemperate and unchaste.

"My brother in the interval was dead, and at the end of the four years my father died too. I was rich enough now – yet Bertha Mason was called by the law and by society a part of me. And I could not rid myself of it by any legal proceedings, for the doctors now discovered that my wife was mad. Jane, you don't like my narrative – shall I defer the rest to another day?"

"No, sir, finish it now – I do earnestly pity you."

"Jane, I approached the verge of despair. Society associated my name and person with her. I yet saw her and heard her daily. She was likely to live as long as I, being as robust in frame as she was infirm in mind. Thus, at the age of twenty-six, I was hopeless.

## Chapter 27

"One night I had been awakened by her yells (since the medical men had pronounced her mad, she had, of course, been shut up). It was a fiery West Indian night. Being unable to sleep in bed, I got up and opened the window. My ears were filled with the curses the maniac still shrieked out. Though two rooms off, I heard every wolfish cry. 'This life,' said I at last, 'is hell.'

"A wind fresh from Europe blew over the ocean and rushed through the open casement; the storm broke and the air grew pure. I then framed and fixed a resolution.

"The sweet wind from Europe was still whispering in the refreshed leaves, and the Atlantic was thundering in glorious liberty. I saw hope revive – and felt regeneration possible. 'Go,' said Hope, 'and live again in Europe. There it is not known what a filthy burden is bound to you. You may take the maniac with you to England. Place her in safety and comfort, shelter her with secrecy and leave her.'

"I acted precisely on this suggestion. My father and brother had not made my marriage known to their acquaintances. To England, then, I conveyed her. A fearful voyage I had with such a monster in the vessel. Glad was I when I at last got her to Thornfield and saw her safely lodged in that third-storey room."

"And what, sir," I asked, while he paused, "did you do when you settled her here? Where did you go?"

"I sought the Continent. My fixed desire was to seek and find a good and intelligent woman, whom I could love: a contrast to the fury I left at Thornfield—"

"But you could not marry, sir."

"I had determined and was convinced that I could and ought. It was not my original intention to deceive, as I have deceived you. I meant to tell my tale plainly, and make my proposals openly, and it appeared to me so absolutely rational that I should be considered free to love and be loved. I never doubted some woman might be found willing and able to understand my case and accept me, in spite of the curse with which I was burdened.

"For ten long years I roved about. Provided with plenty of money, I could choose my own society; no circles were closed against me. Amongst them all I found not one whom I would have asked to marry me. Yet I could not live alone, so I tried the companionship of mistresses. The first I chose was Céline Varens. She had two successors. But, Jane, I see by your face you are not forming a very favourable opinion of me just now."

"Did it not seem to you in the least wrong to live in that way, first with one mistress and then another? You talk of it as a mere matter of course."

"It was with me and I did not like it. It was a grovelling fashion of existence. I should never like to return to it.

"But let me come to the point. Last January, rid of all mistresses, recalled by business, I came back to England. On a frosty winter afternoon, I rode in sight of Thornfield Hall. I expected no peace – no pleasure there. On a stile in Hay Lane I saw a quiet little figure sitting by itself. On the occasion of an accident, it came up and gravely offered me help. I was surly, but it stood by me with strange perseverance and looked and spoke with a sort of authority.

"When once I had pressed the frail shoulder, something new stole into my frame. I heard you come home that night, Jane, though probably you were not aware that I thought of you or watched for you.

"Impatiently I waited for the next evening, when I might summon you to my presence. I made you talk: ere long I found you full of strange contrasts. Your garb and manner were restricted by rule, yet when addressed, you lifted a keen, a daring, eye to my face. There was power in each glance you gave. When plied by close questions, you found ready answers. Very soon you seemed to get used to me; I believe you felt the existence of sympathy between you and your grim master, Jane. Snarl as I would, you showed no surprise or displeasure.

"Thereafter I continued my notice of you. There was something glad in your glance, and genial in your manner, when you conversed. I used to enjoy a chance meeting with you, Jane, at this time. When I stretched my hand out cordially, such bloom and light and bliss rose to your young, wistful features."

# Chapter 27

"Don't talk any more of those days, sir," I interrupted, furtively dashing away some tears from my eyes.

"You see now how the case stands, do you not?" he continued. "After a youth and manhood passed half in misery and half in solitude, I have for the first time found what I can truly love – I have found you. Why are you silent, Jane?"

I was experiencing a terrible ordeal. Him who thus loved me, I absolutely worshipped, and I must renounce love.

"Jane, you understand what I want of you? Just this promise – 'I will be yours, Mr Rochester.'"

"Mr Rochester, I will not be yours."

Another long silence.

"Jane!" recommenced he, with a gentleness that broke me down with grief, "Jane, do you mean to go one way in the world, and to let me go another?"

"I do."

"Jane" (bending towards and embracing me), "do you mean it now?"

"I do."

"And now?" softly kissing my forehead and cheek.

"I do," extricating myself from restraint rapidly and completely.

"Oh, Jane, it would not be wicked to love me."

"It would to obey you."

"Is it better to drive a fellow-creature to despair than to transgress a mere human law?"

This was true, and while he spoke my conscience spoke almost as loud as Feeling, and that clamoured wildly. "Oh, comply!" it said. "Think of his misery. Who in the world cares for you?"

Still indomitable was the reply from my conscience: "I care for myself. I will respect myself. I will keep the law given by God; sanctioned by man."

I retired to the door.

"You are going, Jane?"

"I am going, sir."

"You are leaving me?"

"Yes."

"You will not come? My love, my woe, my prayer, are all nothing to you?"

What unutterable pathos was in his voice! How hard it was to reiterate firmly, "I am going."

He turned away. "Oh, Jane! my hope – my love – my life!" broke in anguish from his lips.

"God bless you, my dear master!" I said. "God keep you from harm and wrong."

He held his arms out, but I evaded the embrace, and at once quitted the room.

"Farewell!" was the cry of my heart as I left him. Despair added, "Farewell for ever!"

That night I never thought to sleep, but a slumber fell on me as soon as I lay down in bed. I waked from a trance-like dream. It was yet night, but July nights are short. Soon after midnight, dawn comes. "It cannot be too early to commence the task I have to fulfil," thought I.

I rose. I was dressed, for I had taken off nothing but my shoes. I knew where to find in my drawers some linen, a locket, a ring. Other articles I made up in a parcel; my purse, containing twenty shillings (all I had), I put in my pocket. I tied on my straw bonnet, pinned my shawl, and stole from my room.

Drearily I wound my way downstairs. I knew what I had to do, and I did it mechanically. I opened the side door of the kitchen, passed out, shut it softly. Dim dawn glimmered in the yard. Through the great gates I departed and was out of Thornfield.

## Chapter 27

A mile off, beyond the fields, lay a road which stretched in the contrary direction to Millcote; a road I had never travelled, but often noticed, and wondered where it led. Thither I bent my steps. I skirted fields, and hedges, and lanes till after sunrise. God must have led me on, for I was weeping wildly as I walked along my solitary way, determined as ever to reach the road.

When I got there, I saw a coach come on. I asked where it was going. The driver named a place a long way off, and where I was sure Mr Rochester had no connections. I asked for what sum he would take me there; he said thirty shillings; I answered I had but twenty; well, he would try to make it do. I entered, was shut in, and it rolled on its way.

Gentle reader, may you never feel what I then felt! May your eyes never shed such stormy tears as poured from mine. May you never appeal to Heaven in prayers so hopeless as in that hour left my lips. For never may you, like me, dread to cause such pain to what you wholly love.

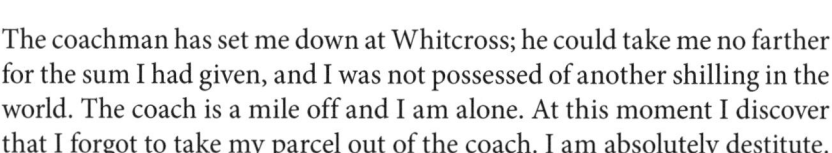

# Chapter 28

The coachman has set me down at Whitcross; he could take me no farther for the sum I had given, and I was not possessed of another shilling in the world. The coach is a mile off and I am alone. At this moment I discover that I forgot to take my parcel out of the coach. I am absolutely destitute.

Whitcross is but a stone pillar set up where four roads meet. Four arms spring from its summit; the nearest town to which these point is ten miles. I see no passengers on these roads. They stretch out east, west, north, and south – white, broad, lonely; they are all cut in the moor, and the heather grows deep and wild to their very verge. I struck straight into the heath. I waded knee-deep in its dark growth and, finding a moss-blackened granite crag in a hidden angle, I sat down under it. High banks of moor were about me. The crag protected my head, and the sky was over that.

Some time passed before I felt tranquil even here, but calmed by the deep silence that reigned as evening declined at nightfall, I took confidence. As yet I had not thought, but now I regained the faculty of reflection.

What was I to do? Where to go? Oh, intolerable questions, when I could do nothing and go nowhere!

I touched the heath; it was dry, and yet warm with the heat of the summer day. I looked at the sky; a kindly star twinkled just above. The dew fell but with softness. No breeze whispered. Nature seemed to me benign and good; I thought she loved me, outcast as I was, and I, who from man could anticipate only mistrust, rejection, insult, clung to her with filial fondness. To-night, at least, I would be her guest. I had one morsel of bread yet, the remnant of a roll I had bought with my last coin. I saw ripe bilberries gleaming here and there, like jet beads in the heath.

## Chapter 28

I gathered a handful and ate them with the bread. Beside the crag the heath was very deep; I lay down in a narrow space.

Night was come, and her planets were risen: a safe, still night. We know that God is everywhere, but certainly we feel His presence most when His works are on the grandest scale spread before us, and it is in the unclouded night-sky, where His worlds wheel their silent course, that we read clearest His infinitude, His omnipotence, His omnipresence. Looking up, I saw the mighty Milky-way. I felt the might and strength of God. Mr Rochester was safe; he was God's, and by God would he be guarded. I nestled to the breast of the hill and ere long in sleep forgot sorrow.

But next day, when the sun filled the earth and sky, I looked round me. What a golden desert this spreading moor! I set out. I followed a road, walking a long time, and when I thought I might yield to the fatigue that almost overpowered me – I heard the chime of a church bell. There, amongst the romantic hills, I saw a hamlet and a spire.

I entered the village. At the bottom of its one street there was a little shop with bread in the window. With that refreshment I could perhaps regain a degree of energy, as without it, it would be difficult to proceed. Had I nothing I could offer in exchange for one of these rolls? I had a small silk handkerchief tied round my throat; I had my gloves. I must try.

I entered the shop. A woman was there. I was seized with shame; I dared not offer her the half-worn gloves, or the creased handkerchief. It would be absurd. I only begged permission to sit down a moment, as I was tired. Disappointed in the expectation of a customer, she pointed to a seat. I sank into it.

In the position of one without a resource, without a friend, without a coin, I must do something.

"Did she know of any place in the neighbourhood where a servant was wanted?"

"Nay; she couldn't say."

"Did the local factory employ women?"

"Nay; it was men's work."

She quickly tired of my questions and, indeed, what claim had I to importune her? I took leave.

I passed up the street, looking as I went at all the houses, but I could discover no pretext to enter any. I rambled round the hamlet. I drew near houses, I left them, and came back again, and again I wandered away, always repelled by the consciousness of having no claim to ask – no right to expect interest in my isolated lot. Meantime, the afternoon advanced, while I thus wandered about like a lost and starving dog.

Much exhausted, and suffering greatly now for want of food, I turned aside into a lane. A pretty little house stood at the top, with a garden before it, exquisitely neat and brilliantly blooming. I stopped at it. What business had I to approach the white door or touch the glittering knocker? Yet I drew near and knocked.

"Can you tell me where I could get employment of any kind?" I asked. "I am a stranger, without acquaintance in this place."

She shook her head, she "was sorry she could give me no information," and the white door closed: quite gently and civilly, but it shut me out.

I could not bear to return to the sordid village, where no aid was visible, but I was so sick, so weak, so gnawed with nature's cravings, that I would have no rest while the vulture, hunger, thus sank beak and talons in my side. Oh, for but a crust! For but one mouthful to allay the pang of famine!

I turned again to the village; I found the shop again, and ventured the request – "Would she give me a roll for this handkerchief?"

She looked at me with suspicion: "Nay, she never sold stuff i' that way. How could she tell where I had got the handkerchief?" she said.

"Would she take my gloves?"

"No! What could she do with them?"

Reader, it is not pleasant to dwell on these details. The moral degradation, combined with the physical suffering, form a distressing a recollection. I blamed none who repulsed me. I felt it was what was to be expected and

# Chapter 28

what could not be helped. An ordinary beggar is frequently an object of suspicion; a well-dressed beggar inevitably so.

I could not hope to get a lodging under a roof and sought it in a nearby wood. But my night was wretched, my rest broken. The ground was damp, the air cold; no sense of safety or tranquillity befriended me. Towards morning it rained. The whole of the following day was wet. Do not ask me, reader, to give a minute account of that day: I was repulsed; I starved; only once did food pass my lips. At the door of a cottage I saw a little girl about to throw cold porridge into a pig trough. "Will you give me that?" I asked. The girl emptied the stiffened mould into my hand, and I devoured it ravenously.

As the wet twilight deepened, "My strength is quite failing me," I said in a soliloquy. "I feel I cannot go much farther. In all likelihood, I should die before morning." My glazed eye wandered over the dim and misty landscape. I saw I had strayed far from the village. It was quite out of sight. I had, once more, drawn near the tract of moorland, and now only a few fields lay between me and the dusky hill. To the hill, then, I turned. I reached it. It remained now only to find a hollow where I could lie down, and feel at least hidden, if not secure.

My eye roved along the moor-edge, vanishing amidst the wildest scenery, when at one dim point, far in among the marshes, a light sprang up. I expected it would soon vanish. But it burnt on, quite steadily, neither receding nor advancing. "It may be a candle in a house," I conjectured, "but it is much too far away and I should but knock at the door to have it shut in my face." But the light was yet there, shining dim but constant through the rain. I tried to walk again. I dragged my exhausted limbs slowly towards it. It led me through a wide bog. Here I fell twice but as often I rose and rallied my faculties. This light was my forlorn hope; I must gain it.

Having crossed the marsh, I saw a track. It led straight up to the light, which now beamed from amidst a clump of trees. A whitish object gleamed before me: it was a gate – a wicket. It moved on its hinges as I touched it.

Entering the gate and passing the shrubs, the silhouette of a house rose to view, black, low, and rather long. There, from the lozenged panes of a very small latticed window, shot out the friendly gleam and I could see all within. I could see clearly a room with a sanded floor, clean scoured, a clock, a dresser of walnut, with pewter plates ranged in rows, reflecting a glowing peat-fire. The candle, whose ray had been my beacon, burnt on the table and by its light an elderly woman, rough-looking, was knitting. Near the hearth, amidst the rosy peace and warmth suffusing it, two young, graceful women sat, one in a low rocking-chair, the other on a lower stool. Both wore deep mourning; a large old pointer dog rested its massive head on the knee of one girl – in the lap of the other was cushioned a black cat.

A strange place was this humble kitchen for such occupants! Who were they? They could not be the daughters of the elderly person at the table, for she looked like a rustic and they were all delicacy and cultivation. The ladies were both fair complexioned and slenderly made; both possessed faces full of distinction and intelligence. One had pale brown locks parted and braided smooth; the other's duskier tresses covered her neck with thick curls. The clock struck ten. The ladies rose. They seemed about to withdraw to the parlour. I groped out the door and knocked at it hesitatingly. The old servant opened.

"What do you want?" she inquired, in a voice of surprise, as she surveyed me by the light of the candle she held.

"May I speak to your mistresses?" I said.

"What is your business here at this hour?"

"I want a night's shelter, and a morsel of bread to eat."

Distrust appeared in her face. "I'll give you a piece of bread," she said, after a pause.

"But where shall I go if you drive me away? What shall I do? I must die if I am turned away."

Here the honest but inflexible servant clapped the door to and bolted it within.

A pang of exquisite suffering – a throe of true despair – rent and heaved my heart. Worn out, indeed, I was. Not another step could I stir. I sank on the wet doorstep. Alas, this isolation – this banishment from my kind!

## Chapter 28

"I can but die," I said, "and I believe in God. Let me try to wait His will in silence."

These words I not only thought, but uttered.

"All men must die," said a voice quite close at hand, "but all are not condemned to meet a lingering and premature doom, such as yours would be if you perished here of want."

"Who or what speaks?" I asked, terrified at the unexpected sound. With a loud long knock, the new-comer appealed to the door.

"Is it you, Mr St John?" cried the old servant.

"Yes – yes, Hannah, open quickly."

"There has been a beggar-woman– laid down there. Get up! For shame! Move off, I say!"

"Hush, Hannah! You have done your duty in excluding, now let me do mine in admitting her. Young woman, rise." With difficulty I obeyed him.

Presently I stood within that clean, bright kitchen. The two ladies, their brother, Mr St John, the old servant, were all gazing at me.

"St John, who is it?" I heard one ask.

"I cannot tell Mary; I found her at the door," was the reply.

"Is she ill, or only famished?"

"Famished, I think. Diana, is that milk? Give it me, and a piece of bread."

Diana broke some bread, dipped it in milk, and put it to my lips. Her face was near mine. "Try to eat."

"Yes – try," repeated Mary, gently.

"Not too much at first," said the brother; "she has had enough." And he withdrew the cup of milk and the plate of bread. "Ask her name."

I felt I could speak, and I answered – "My name is Jane Elliott."

"And where do you live? Where are your friends?"

I was silent.

"Can we send for anyone you know?"

I shook my head.

"Hannah," said Mr St John at last, "let her sit there at present. Mary and Diana, let us go into the parlour and talk the matter over." They withdrew.

Ere long, with the servant's aid, I contrived to mount a staircase. My dripping clothes were removed; soon a warm, dry bed received me. I experienced a glow of grateful joy, and slept.

# Chapter 29

The recollection of about three days and nights succeeding this is very dim in my mind. Hannah, the servant, was my most frequent visitor. Diana and Mary appeared in the chamber once or twice a day. Never once in their dialogues did I hear a syllable of regret at the hospitality they had extended to me, or of suspicion of myself. I was comforted.

Mr St John came but once; he looked at me and said my state of lethargy was the result of reaction from excessive fatigue. He said every nerve had been overstrained in some way, and the whole system must sleep a while. There was no disease. He imagined my recovery would be rapid enough when once commenced. He added, "She looks sensible, but not at all handsome."

"She is so ill, St John," responded Diana.

"Ill or well, she would always be plain. The grace and harmony of beauty are quite wanting in those features."

On the fourth day I felt comparatively strong and revived. I wished to rise. On a chair by the bedside were all my own things, clean and dry. The traces of the bog were removed from my black silk frock; the creases left by the wet smoothed out. My shoes and stockings were purified and rendered presentable. My clothes hung loose on me, for I was much wasted, but I covered deficiencies with a shawl, and once more, was clean and respectable looking.

I crept down a stone staircase to a narrow low passage, and found my way presently to the kitchen.

It was full of the fragrance of new bread and the warmth of a generous fire. Hannah was baking. Hannah had been cold and stiff, indeed, at the first; latterly she had begun to relent a little and when she saw me come in tidy and well-dressed, she even smiled. She pointed to the rocking-chair – I took it. She bustled about, examining me every now and then with the corner of her eye.

"Are you book-learned?" she inquired presently.

"Yes, very."

"But you've never been to a boarding-school?"

"I was at a boarding-school eight years."

She opened her eyes wide. "Ye've not been used to sarvant's wark, I see by your hands," she remarked. "Happen ye've been a dressmaker?"

"No, you are wrong. And now, never mind what I have been, but tell me the name of the house where we are."

"Some calls it Moor House."

"And the gentleman who lives here, Mr St John?"

"Nay, he doesn't live here. He has his own parish at Morton."

"He is a parson."

"Old Mr Rivers lived here, and his father, and grandfather, and great-grandfather afore him. St John is like his kirstened name."

"And his sisters are called Diana and Mary Rivers?"

"Yes."

"Their father is dead?"

"Dead three weeks sin' of a stroke."

"They have no mother?"

"The mistress has been dead this mony a year. I nursed them all three."

Hannah was evidently fond of talking. While she made the paste for the pies, she proceeded to give me sundry details about her deceased master and mistress, and "the childer," as she called the young people.

Old Mr Rivers, she said, was a plain man enough, but a gentleman, and of as ancient a family as could be found. The mistress was a great reader and studied a deal, and the "bairns" had taken after her. They had liked learning, all three. Mr St John, when he grew up, went to college and is a parson, and the girls, as soon as they left school, sought places as governesses, for their father had some years ago lost a great deal of money, and as he was not rich enough to give them fortunes, they must provide for themselves. They had lived very little at home for a long while, but they did so like Marsh End and Morton, and all these moors and hills about.

The two ladies and their brother returned in time for tea. Mr St John, when he saw me, merely bowed and passed through; Mary expressed the pleasure she felt in seeing me well enough to be able to come down; Diana took my hand, made me rise and led me into the inner room.

"Sit there," she said, placing me on the sofa, "while we take our things off and get the tea ready."

She closed the door, leaving me alone with Mr St John, who sat opposite, a book in his hand. Mr St John – sitting still, keeping his eyes fixed on the page he perused – was easy enough to examine. Had he been a statue instead of a man, he could not have been easier. He was young – perhaps from twenty-eight to thirty – tall and slender. His face riveted the eye. It was like a Greek face, very pure in outline: quite a straight, classic nose; quite an Athenian mouth and chin. It is seldom, indeed, an English face comes so near the antique models as did his. He might well be a little shocked at the irregularity of my lineaments, his own being so harmonious. His eyes were large and blue, with brown lashes; his high forehead, colourless as ivory, was partially streaked over by careless locks of fair hair.

This is a gentle delineation, is it not, reader? Yet he whom it describes scarcely impressed one with the idea of a gentle, a yielding, or even of a placid nature. Calm as he now sat, there was something about his nostril, his mouth, his brow, which, to my perceptions, indicated elements within either restless, or hard, or eager. He did not speak to me one word, nor even direct to me one glance.

Diana, as she passed in and out, in the course of preparing tea, brought me a little cake, baked on the top of the oven.

"Eat that now," she said, "you must be hungry."

I did not refuse it, for my appetite was awakened and keen. Mr Rivers now closed his book, approached the table, and, as he took a seat, fixed his blue pictorial-looking eyes full on me. There was a directness, a searching, decided steadfastness in his gaze now, which told that intention, and not diffidence, had hitherto kept it averted from the stranger.

"You are very hungry," he said.

"I trust I shall not eat long at your expense, sir," was my very clumsily-contrived answer.

"No," he said coolly, "when you have indicated to us the residence of your friends, we can write to them, and you may be restored to home."

"That, I must plainly tell you, is out of my power to do, being absolutely without home and friends."

The three looked at me, but not distrustfully. I felt there was no suspicion in their glances, more of curiosity.

"Do you mean to say," he asked, "that you are completely isolated from every connection?"

"I do. Not a tie links me to any living thing. Not a claim do I possess to admittance under any roof in England."

"You have never been married? You are a spinster?"

"I am near nineteen but I am not married. No."

"Where did you last reside?" he now asked.

"The name of the place where, and of the person with whom I lived, is my secret," I replied concisely.

"Yet if I know nothing about you or your history, I cannot help you," he said. "And you need help, do you not?"

"Mr Rivers," I said, turning to him, and looking at him, as he looked at me, openly and without diffidence, "you and your sisters have done me a great service – the greatest man can do his fellow-being; you have rescued me, by your noble hospitality, from death. I will tell you as much of the history of the wanderer you have harboured as I can tell without compromising my own peace of mind – my own security, moral and physical, and that of others.

"I am an orphan, the daughter of a clergyman. My parents died before I could know them. I was brought up a dependent, and educated in a charitable institution – Lowood Orphan Asylum. I left Lowood nearly a year since to become a private governess. I obtained a good situation and was happy. This place I was obliged to leave four days before I came here. The reason of my departure I cannot and ought not to explain. It would be useless, dangerous, and would sound incredible. No blame attached to me. To this neighbourhood, then, I came, quite destitute. I slept two nights in the open air, when brought by hunger, exhaustion, and despair almost to the last gasp, you, Mr Rivers, took me under the shelter of your roof, and I owe a large debt to your evangelical charity."

"Don't make her talk any more now, St John," said Diana as I paused. "Come to the sofa and sit down now, Miss Elliott."

I gave an involuntary half start at hearing the alias. I had forgotten my new name. Mr Rivers, whom nothing seemed to escape, noticed it at once.

"You said your name was Jane Elliott?" he observed.

"I did say so, but it is not my real name."

"Your real name you will not give?"

"No. I fear discovery above all things."

"You are quite right, I am sure," said Diana. "Now do, brother, let her be at peace a while."

But when St John had mused a few moments he recommenced.

"You would wish, I see, to be independent of us?"

"I do. I have already said so. Show me how to work, or how to seek work, that is all I now ask. Then let me go, if it be but to the meanest cottage, but till then, allow me to stay here."

"Indeed, you shall stay here," said Diana, putting her white hand on my head.

"You shall," repeated Mary, in the tone of undemonstrative sincerity.

"I will be a dressmaker, a plain-workwoman; I will be a servant, a nurse-girl, if I can be no better," I answered.

"Right," said Mr St John, quite coolly. "if such is your spirit, I promise to aid you."

He resumed the book with which he had been occupied before tea. I soon withdrew, for I had talked and sat up as long as my present strength would permit.

# Chapter 30

The more I knew of the inmates of Moor House, the better I liked them. I could join with Diana and Mary in all their occupations, converse with them and aid them when and where they would allow me.

I liked to read what they liked to read. What they enjoyed, delighted me. They loved their sequestered home. I, too, in the grey, small, antique structure, with its low roof, its latticed casements, its garden, dark with yew and holly – and where no flowers but of the hardiest species would bloom – found a charm both potent and permanent.

They were both more accomplished and better read than I was, but with eagerness I followed in the path of knowledge they had trodden before me. I devoured the books they lent me; then it was full satisfaction to discuss with them in the evening what I had perused during the day. Thought fitted thought, opinion met opinion. We coincided, in short, perfectly. Thus occupied, and mutually entertained, days passed like hours, and weeks like days.

As to Mr St John, the intimacy which had arisen so naturally and rapidly between me and his sisters did not extend to him. One reason was that he was comparatively seldom at home. A large proportion of his time appeared devoted to visiting the sick and poor among the scattered population of his parish. Rain or fair, he would, when his hours of morning study were over, go out on his mission of love or duty – I scarcely know in which light he regarded it.

But besides his frequent absences, there was another barrier to friendship with him: he seemed of a reserved, an abstracted, and even of a brooding nature. Zealous in his ministerial labours, blameless in his life and habits, he yet did not appear to enjoy that mental serenity, that inward content, which should be the reward of every sincere Christian. I think, moreover, that Nature was not to him that treasury of delight it was to his sisters, and never did he seem to roam the moors for the sake of their soothing silence, never seek out or dwell upon the thousand peaceful delights they could yield.

I first got an idea of the calibre of his mind when I heard him preach in his church at Morton. When he had done, instead of feeling better, calmer, more enlightened by his discourse, I experienced an inexpressible sadness, for it seemed to me that the eloquence to which I had been listening had sprung from a deep disappointment. I was sure St John Rivers – pure-lived, conscientious, zealous as he was – had not yet found that peace of God which passeth all understanding.

Meantime a month was gone. Diana and Mary were soon to leave Moor House, and return as governesses in a large, fashionable, south-of-England city, where each held a situation in families by whose wealthy and haughty members they were regarded only as humble dependents. Mr St John had said nothing to me yet about the employment he had promised to obtain for me, yet it became urgent that I should have a vocation of some kind.

One morning, being left alone with him a few minutes in the parlour, I ventured to approach. Looking up as I drew near – "You have a question to ask of me?" he said.

"Yes; I wish to know whether you have heard of any service I can offer myself to undertake? Diana and Mary will go in three days now."

"Yes, and when they go, I shall return to the parsonage at Morton. Hannah will accompany me, and this old house will be shut up."

He paused. There seemed a reluctance to continue. "Let me frankly tell you," he said, "I have nothing eligible or profitable to suggest. Since I am myself poor and obscure, I can offer you but a service of poverty and obscurity. You may even think it degrading – but I consider that no service degrades which can better our race."

"Do explain," I urged, when he halted.

"Morton, when I came to it two years ago, had no school; the children of the poor were excluded from every hope of progress. I established

## Chapter 30

one for boys. I mean now to open a second school for girls. I have hired a building, with a cottage of two rooms attached to it for the mistress's house. Her salary will be thirty pounds a year; her house is already furnished, very simply, by the kindness of a lady, Miss Oliver, the only daughter of the sole rich man in my parish. Will you be its mistress?"

In truth it was humble, but then it was sheltered, and I wanted a safe asylum. It was plodding, but then, compared with that of a governess in a rich house, it was independent, and the fear of servitude with strangers entered my soul like iron. It was not ignoble – not unworthy – not mentally degrading. I made my decision.

"I thank you for the proposal, Mr Rivers, and I accept it with all my heart."

"But you comprehend me?" he said. "It is a village school. Your scholars will be only poor girls – cottagers' children – at the best, farmers' daughters. Knitting, sewing, reading, writing, ciphering, will be all you will have to teach. You know what you undertake?"

"I do."

He now smiled, pleased and deeply gratified.

"I will go to my house to-morrow, and open the school, if you like, next week."

"Very well; so be it."

He rose, and standing still, he shook his head.

"You will not stay at Morton long. No, no!"

"Why? What is your reason for saying so?"

"I read it in your eye."

"I am not ambitious."

He started at the word "ambitious."

"Who is ambitious? I know I am, but how did you find it out? I am sure you cannot long be content to pass your leisure in solitude and to devote your working hours to a monotonous labour wholly void of stimulus, any more than I can be content," he added.

He left the room. In this brief hour I had learnt more of him than in the whole previous month.

Diana and Mary Rivers became more sad and silent as the day approached for leaving their brother and their home. Diana intimated that this would be a different parting from any they had ever yet known. It would probably, as far as St John was concerned, be a parting for years; it might be a parting for life.

"We are now without father. We shall soon be without home and brother," Mary murmured.

At that moment a little accident supervened, to add to their distresses. St John entered.

"Our uncle John is dead," said he.

Both the sisters seemed struck, not shocked or appalled. The tidings appeared in their eyes rather momentous than afflicting.

"Dead?" repeated Diana. "And what then?" she demanded, in a low voice.

"What then? Why – nothing. Read," he replied, maintaining a marble immobility of feature.

He threw the letter into her lap. She glanced over it and handed it to Mary.

"At any rate, it makes us no worse off than we were before," remarked Mary.

"Only it forces rather strongly on the mind the picture of what might have been," said Mr Rivers.

Diana then turned to me.

"Jane," she said, "you will think us hard-hearted beings not to be more moved at the death of so near a relation as an uncle, but we have never seen him or known him. He was my mother's brother. My father and he quarrelled long ago. By his advice my father risked most of his property in the speculation that ruined him. My uncle afterwards realised a

## Chapter 30

fortune of twenty thousand pounds. He was never married and had no near kindred but ourselves and one other person, not more closely related than we. My father cherished the idea that he would atone for his error by leaving his possessions to us. That letter informs us that he has bequeathed every penny to the other relation. He had a right, of course, to do as he pleased. Mary and I would have esteemed ourselves rich with a thousand pounds each and to St John such a sum would have been valuable, for the good it would have enabled him to do."

This explanation given, the subject was dropped.

The next day I left Marsh End for Morton. The day after, Diana and Mary quitted it. In a week, Mr Rivers and Hannah repaired to the parsonage, and so the old grange was abandoned.

# Chapter 31

My home, then, is a cottage: a little room with whitewashed walls and a sanded floor, containing four painted chairs and a table, a clock, a cupboard, with two or three plates and dishes, and a set of tea-things. Above, a chamber of the same dimensions as the kitchen, with a bed and chest of drawers, too large to be filled with my scanty wardrobe.

It is evening. I am sitting alone on the hearth. This morning, the village school opened. I had twenty scholars. Only three of the number can read, none write. Several knit, and a few sew a little. They speak with the broadest accent of the district and I have a difficulty in understanding. Some of them are unmannered, as well as ignorant, but others have a wish to learn. I must not forget that the germs of native excellence, refinement, intelligence, kind feeling, are as likely to exist in their hearts as in those of the best-born.

Was I content, during the hours I passed in the humble schoolroom this morning and afternoon? I must reply: no. I felt desolate to a degree – I felt degraded. I was dismayed at the ignorance, the poverty, the coarseness of all round me. But I shall strive to overcome these feelings. In a few months, it is possible, the happiness of seeing progress and a change for the better in my scholars may substitute gratification for disgust.

Meantime, let me ask myself one question: Which is better? To have surrendered to temptation; listened to passion; made no painful effort – no struggle – but to have been now living in France amongst the luxuries of a pleasure villa, Mr Rochester's mistress? He would have loved me well for a while. He did love me – no one will ever love me so again. Whether is it better, I ask, to be a slave in a fool's paradise at Marseilles – fevered with delusive bliss one hour – suffocating with the bitterest tears of

# Chapter 31

remorse and shame the next – or to be a village-schoolmistress, free and honest, in the healthy heart of England?

I rose, went to my door, and looked at the sunset and at the quiet fields before my cottage. While I looked, I was surprised to find myself weeping. I hid my eyes and leant my head against the stone frame of my door, but soon a slight noise near the wicket which shut in my tiny garden from the meadow beyond it made me look up. St John himself leant upon it with folded arms, his brow knit, his gaze, grave almost to displeasure, fixed on me. I asked him to come in.

"No, I cannot stay. I have only brought you a little parcel my sisters left for you."

He examined my face as I came near; the traces of tears were doubtless very visible upon it.

"Have you found your first day's work harder than you expected?" he asked.

"Oh, no! On the contrary, I think in time I shall get on with my scholars very well."

"But perhaps your accommodations—"

I interrupted, "My cottage is clean and weather-proof. All I see has made me thankful, not despondent. Besides, five weeks ago I had nothing – I was an outcast; now I have acquaintance, a home, a business. I wonder at the bounty of my lot."

"But you feel solitude?"

"I have hardly had time yet to grow lonely."

"Very well, but I counsel you to resist every temptation which would incline you to look back. Pursue your present career steadily, for some months at least. It is hard work to control the workings of inclination and turn the bent of nature, but that it may be done I know, from experience.

"A year ago I was myself intensely miserable, because I thought I had made a mistake in entering the ministry; its uniform duties wearied me to death. I burnt for the more active life of the world – for the destiny of an artist, author, orator – anything rather than that of a priest. I considered my life was so wretched, it must be changed, or I must die. After a season of darkness and struggling, light broke and relief fell. God had an errand for me which needed skill and strength, courage and eloquence: a missionary I resolved to be.

"From that moment my state of mind changed, and since my father's death I have not a legitimate obstacle to contend with, only a last conflict with human weakness, in which I have vowed that I *will* overcome – and I leave Europe for the East."

Both he and I had our backs towards the path leading up to the wicket. We had heard no step on that grass-grown track. The water running in the vale was the one lulling sound. We might well then start when a gay voice, sweet as a silver bell, exclaimed –

"Good evening, Mr Rivers."

Mr Rivers had started at the first of those musical accents, as if a thunderbolt had split a cloud over his head. He turned, with measured deliberation. A vision, as it seemed to me, had risen at his side. There appeared, within three feet of him, a form clad in pure white – a youthful, graceful form, full, yet fine in contour – and there bloomed under his glance a face of perfect beauty. Perfect beauty is a strong expression, but no charm was wanting, no defect was perceptible. The young girl had regular and delicate lineaments: eyes shaped and coloured as we see them in lovely pictures, large, and dark, and full; the long and shadowy eyelash which encircles a fine eye; the white smooth forehead; the cheek oval, fresh, and smooth; the lips, fresh too, ruddy, healthy, sweetly formed; the even and gleaming teeth without flaw; the small dimpled chin; the ornament of rich, plenteous tresses – all advantages, in short, which, combined, realise the ideal of beauty, were fully hers.

What did St John Rivers think of this earthly angel? He had already withdrawn his eye from her and was looking at a humble tuft of daisies which grew by the wicket.

"A lovely evening, but late for you to be out alone," he said, as he crushed the snowy heads of the closed flowers with his foot.

"Oh, I only came home this afternoon. Papa told me you had opened your school, and that the new mistress was come, and so I put on my bonnet after tea and ran up the valley to see her. This is she?" pointing to me.

"It is," said St John.

"Do you think you shall like Morton?" she asked of me.

"I hope I shall."

"Did you find your scholars as attentive as you expected?"

"Quite."

"Do you like your house?"

"Very much."

"Have I furnished it nicely?"

"Very nicely, indeed."

This then, I thought, is Miss Oliver, the heiress; favoured, it seems, in the gifts of fortune, as well as in those of nature!

"I shall come up and help you to teach sometimes," she added. "It will be a change, and I like a change. Mr Rivers, I have been so gay during my stay away. Last night, I was dancing till two o'clock with the officers – the most agreeable men in the world!"

It seemed to me that Mr St John's under lip protruded, and his upper lip curled a moment, his face unusually stern and square as the laughing girl gave him this information. He lifted his gaze, too, from the daisies, and turned it on her. An unsmiling, a searching, a meaning gaze it was. She answered it with a second laugh, and laughter well became her youth, her roses, her dimples, her bright eyes.

I saw a glow rise to that master's face. I saw his solemn eye melt with sudden fire, and flicker with resistless emotion. His chest heaved once, as if his large heart, weary of constriction, had expanded, despite the will, and made a vigorous bound for liberty. But he curbed it, I think, as a resolute rider would curb a rearing steed. He responded neither by word nor movement to the gentle advances made him.

"Papa says you never come to see us now," continued Miss Oliver, looking up. "You are quite a stranger. He is alone this evening. Will you return with me and visit him?"

"It is not a seasonable hour to intrude on Mr Oliver," answered St John.

"Not a seasonable hour! But I declare it is. It is just the hour when papa most wants company. Now, Mr Rivers, do come. Why are you so very shy, and so very sombre?"

"Not to-night, Miss Rosamond, not to-night."

Mr St John spoke almost like an automaton; himself only knew the effort it cost him thus to refuse.

"Well, if you are so obstinate, I will leave you, for I dare not stay any longer. The dew begins to fall. Good evening!"

She held out her hand. He just touched it. "Good evening!" he repeated, in a voice low and hollow as an echo.

She turned twice to gaze after him as she tripped fairy-like down the field. He, as he strode firmly across, never turned at all.

# Chapter 32

I continued the labours of the village-school. It was truly hard work at first, but the rapidity of my scholars' progress was surprising, and an honest and happy pride I took in it. Their parents also loaded me with attentions. I felt I became a favourite in the neighbourhood. Whenever I went out, I heard on all sides cordial salutations, and was welcomed with friendly smiles. To live amidst general regard, though it be but the regard of working people, is like "sitting in sunshine, calm and sweet"; serene inward feelings bud and bloom under the ray.

At this period of my life, my heart far oftener swelled with thankfulness than sank with dejection. And yet, reader, in the midst of this calm, I used to rush into strange dreams at night, dreams in which I still again and again met Mr Rochester, and then the sense of being in his arms, hearing his voice, meeting his eye, touching his hand and cheek, loving him, being loved by him – the hope of passing a lifetime at his side, would be renewed, with all its first force and fire. Then I awoke.

Rosamond Oliver kept her word in coming to visit me. Her call at the school generally came at the hour when Mr Rivers was engaged in giving his daily religious instruction. Keenly, I fear, did the eye of the visitress pierce the young pastor's heart. When she appeared, his cheek would glow, and his marble-seeming features, though they refused to relax, changed indescribably.

Of course, she knew her power. When she addressed him, and smiled gaily, encouragingly, even fondly in his face, his hand would tremble and his eye burn. He seemed to say, with his sad and resolute look, if he did not say it with his lips, "I love you, and I know you prefer me. If I offered my heart, I believe you would accept it. But that heart is already laid on a sacred altar." And then she would pout like a disappointed child and turn from his aspect. St John, no doubt, would have given the world to follow, recall, retain her, when she thus left him, but he would not relinquish, for the paradise of her love, one hope of the true, eternal Heaven.

Miss Oliver honoured me with frequent visits to my cottage. I had learnt her whole character, which was without mystery or disguise. One evening, she discovered my drawing-materials and some sketches, including a pencil-head of one of my scholars. She was first transfixed with surprise, and then electrified with delight.

"Had I done these pictures? Would I sketch a portrait of her, to show to papa?"

"With pleasure," I replied, and I felt a thrill of artist-delight at the idea of copying from so perfect and radiant a model.

She made such a report of me to her father, that Mr Oliver insisted on my coming to spend an evening at Vale Hall. I went. I found it a large, handsome residence, showing abundant evidences of wealth in the proprietor. Mr Oliver expressed, in strong terms, his approval of what I had done in Morton school and was very kind to me. The sketch of Rosamond's portrait pleased him highly; he said I must make a finished picture of it.

Mr Oliver spoke of the Rivers family with great respect. He accounted it a pity that so fine and talented a young man as Mr St John Rivers should have formed the design of going out as a missionary; it was quite throwing a valuable life away. It appeared, then, that her father would throw no obstacle in the way of Rosamond's union with St John. Mr Oliver evidently regarded the young clergyman's good birth, old name, and sacred profession as sufficient compensation for the want of fortune.

Some weeks later, I was absorbed in the execution of Rosamond Oliver's miniature, when, after one rapid tap, my door unclosed, admitting St John Rivers.

"I am come to see how you are," he said. "Not, I hope, in thought? No, that is well. While you draw you will not feel lonely."

# Chapter 32

St John stooped to examine my drawing. His tall figure sprang erect again with a start. He said nothing. I knew his thoughts well and could read his heart plainly.

"Is this portrait like?" I asked bluntly.

"A well-executed picture," he said, "very soft, clear colouring; very graceful and correct drawing."

"Yes, yes. But what of the resemblance? Who is it like?"

Mastering some hesitation, he answered, "Miss Oliver, I presume."

"Of course. And would it comfort, or would it wound you to have a similar painting? Tell me that. When you are at Madagascar, or at the Cape, or in India, would it be a consolation to have that memento in your possession, or would the sight of it bring distress?"

"That I should like to have it is certain. Whether it would be judicious or wise is another question."

"As far as I can see, it would be more judicious if you were to take to yourself the original at once. She likes you, I am sure," said I, "and her father respects you. You ought to marry her."

"Does she like me?" he asked.

"Certainly! She talks of you continually; there is no subject she enjoys so much."

"It is very pleasant to hear this," he said, "very. Go on for another quarter of an hour." And he actually took out his watch and laid it upon the table to measure the time.

"But where is the use of going on," I asked, "when you are probably preparing some iron blow of contradiction, or forging a fresh chain to fetter your heart?"

"Fancy me yielding and melting, as I am doing; human love rising like a freshly opened fountain in my mind. Now I see myself stretched on an ottoman at my bride Rosamond Oliver's feet. She is mine – I am hers – Hush! say nothing – my heart is full of delight – my senses are entranced – let the time I marked pass in peace."

I humoured him. The watch ticked on. He breathed fast and low. I stood silent. Amidst this hush the quartet sped; he replaced the watch, laid the picture down, rose, and stood on the hearth.

"Now," said he, "that little space was given to delusion. While I love Rosamond Oliver so wildly, I experience at the same time a consciousness that she would not make me a good wife, that she is not the partner suited to me, that I should discover this within a year after marriage and that to twelve months' rapture would succeed a lifetime of regret. This I know. Rosamond a sufferer, a labourer, a female apostle? Rosamond a missionary's wife? No!"

"But you need not be a missionary. You might relinquish that scheme."

"Relinquish! What! My vocation? My great work? My foundation laid on earth for a mansion in heaven? It is what I have to look forward to, and to live for."

After a considerable pause, I said, "And Miss Oliver? Are her disappointment and sorrow of no interest to you?"

"In less than a month, my image will be effaced from her heart. She will forget me and will marry, probably, someone who will make her far happier than I should do."

"You tremble and become flushed whenever Miss Oliver enters the schoolroom."

Again, the surprised expression crossed his face. He had not imagined that a woman would dare to speak so to a man.

"You are original," said he, "and not timid. When I colour, and when I shake before Miss Oliver, I do not pity myself. I scorn the weakness. Know me to be what I am – a cold, hard man."

Having said this, he took his hat, which lay on the table beside my palette. Once more he looked at the portrait.

"She is lovely," he murmured. "She is well named the Rose of the World, indeed!"

He drew over the picture the sheet of thin paper on which I was accustomed to rest my hand in painting. What he suddenly saw on this blank paper, it was impossible to tell, but something caught his eye. He took it up with a snatch; he looked at the edge, then shot a glance at me, inexpressibly peculiar. A glance that seemed to take and make note of every point in my shape, face, and dress, for it traversed all, quick, keen as lightning.

"What is the matter?" I asked.

"Nothing in the world," was the reply and, replacing the paper, I saw him dexterously tear a narrow slip from the margin. It disappeared in his glove and, with one hasty nod and "good-afternoon," he vanished.

I, in my turn, scrutinised the paper, but saw nothing. I pondered the mystery a minute or two, but being certain it could not be of much moment, I soon forgot it.

# Chapter 33

When Mr St John went, it was beginning to snow; the whirling storm continued all night. The next day a keen wind brought fresh falls; by twilight the valley was drifted up and almost impassable. I had closed my shutter, lit a candle and was beginning to read when I heard a noise. The wind, I thought, shook the door. No. It was St John Rivers, who came in and stood before me, the cloak that covered his tall figure all white as a glacier.

"Any ill news?" I demanded. "Has anything happened?"

"No. How very easily alarmed you are!" he answered. He stamped the snow from his boots and approached the fire. "I have had hard work to get here," he observed, as he warmed his hands over the flame. "One drift took me up to the waist."

"But why are you come?" I asked.

"Simply to have a little talk with you. Since yesterday I have experienced a tale which has been half-told, and am impatient to hear the sequel."

He sat down and slowly moved his finger over his upper lip. His eye dwelt dreamily on the glowing grate. He took out a pocket-book, thence produced a letter, which he read in silence, folded it, put it back, and relapsed into meditation.

"Leave your book a moment, and come a little nearer the fire," he finally said.

"Twenty years ago, a poor curate – never mind his name – fell in love with a rich man's daughter. She fell in love with him, and married him, against the advice of all her friends. Before two years passed, the pair were both dead. They left a daughter who was reared by an aunt, called

## Chapter 33

Mrs Reed of Gateshead. You start – did you hear a noise? I daresay it is only a rat scrambling along the rafters of the schoolroom. Mrs Reed kept the orphan ten years, but at the end of that time she transferred it to a place you know – being no other than Lowood School, where you so long resided yourself. It seems her career there was very honourable. From a pupil, she became a teacher, like yourself – really it strikes me there are parallel points in her history and yours. She left it to be a governess – there, again, your fates were the same; she undertook the education of the ward of a certain Mr Rochester."

"Mr Rivers!" I interrupted.

"I can guess your feelings," he said, "but restrain them for a while. I have nearly finished; hear me to the end. Of Mr Rochester's character I know nothing, but the one fact that he professed to offer honourable marriage to this young girl, and that at the very altar she discovered he had a wife yet alive, though a lunatic. The governess left Thornfield Hall in the night; every search after her was in vain. Yet that she should be found is become a matter of serious urgency. Advertisements have been put in all the papers. I myself have received a letter from one Mr Briggs, a solicitor, communicating the details I have just imparted. Is it not an odd tale?"

"Just tell me this," said I, "and since you know so much, you surely can tell it me – what of Mr Rochester? How and where is he? Is he well?"

"I am ignorant of all concerning Mr Rochester. You should rather ask the name of the governess – the nature of the event which requires her appearance."

"Did no one go to Thornfield Hall, then? Did no one see Mr Rochester?"

"I suppose not."

"But they wrote to him?"

"Of course."

"And what did he say? Who has his letters?"

"Mr Briggs intimates that the answer to his application was not from Mr Rochester, but from a lady. It is signed 'Alice Fairfax.'"

I felt cold and dismayed. My worst fears then were probably true; he had in all probability left England and rushed in reckless desperation to some former haunt on the Continent. Oh, my poor master – once almost my husband!

"He must have been a bad man," observed Mr Rivers.

"You don't know him – don't pronounce an opinion upon him," I said, with warmth.

"Very well," he answered quietly, "I have my tale to finish. Since you won't ask the governess's name, I must tell it of my own accord. Stay! I have it here."

And the pocket-book was again deliberately produced. From one of its compartments was extracted a shabby slip of paper, hastily torn off. I recognised the ravished margin of the portrait-cover. He got up, held it close to my eyes and I read, in my own handwriting, the words 'JANE EYRE'.

"Briggs wrote to me of a Jane Eyre," he said. "The advertisements demanded a Jane Eyre. I knew a Jane Elliott. I confess I had my suspicions, but it was only yesterday afternoon they were at once resolved into certainty. You own the name?"

"Yes – yes, but where is Mr Briggs? He perhaps knows more of Mr Rochester than you do."

"Briggs is in London. I should doubt his knowing anything at all about Mr Rochester. It is not in Mr Rochester he is interested. You do not inquire what Mr Briggs wanted with you."

"Well, what did he want?"

"Merely to tell you that your uncle, Mr Eyre of Madeira, is dead, that he has left you all his property, and that you are now rich – merely that – nothing more."

"I! Rich?"

"Yes, you, rich – quite an heiress."

## Chapter 33

Silence succeeded. Here was a new card turned up! It is a fine thing, reader, to be lifted in a moment to wealth – a very fine thing, but not a matter one can comprehend, or consequently enjoy, all at once. Besides, my uncle I had heard was dead – my only relative. I had cherished the hope of one day seeing him; now, I never should. And then this money came only to me, not to me and a rejoicing family, but to my isolated self.

"Perhaps now you will ask how much you are worth?" said Mr Rivers.

"How much am I worth?"

"Oh, a trifle! Nothing of course to speak of – twenty thousand pounds, I think they say."

"Twenty thousand pounds?"

Here was a new stunner – I had been calculating on four or five thousand. This news actually took my breath for a moment.

"It is a large sum – don't you think there is a mistake?" said I.

"No mistake at all."

"Perhaps you have read the figures wrong – it may be two thousand!"

"It is written in letters, not figures – twenty thousand."

Mr Rivers rose now and put his cloak on.

"If it were not such a very wild night," he said, "I would send Hannah down to keep you company."

He was lifting the latch. A sudden thought occurred to me.

"Stop one minute!" I cried.

"Well?"

"It puzzles me to know why Mr Briggs wrote to you about me, or how he could fancy that you, living in such an out-of-the-way place, had the power to aid in my discovery."

"Oh! I am a clergyman," he said, "and the clergy are often appealed to about odd matters." Again the latch rattled.

"No; that does not satisfy me!" I exclaimed. And indeed there was something in the hasty reply which piqued my curiosity more than ever.

"It is a very strange piece of business," I added; "I must know more about it."

"Another time."

"No! To-night! – to-night!" and as he turned from the door, I placed myself between it and him. He looked rather embarrassed.

"You certainly shall not go till you have told me all," I said.

"I would rather not just now."

"You shall! You must!"

"Well, then," he said, "I yield. Besides, you must know some day – as well now as later. Your name is Jane Eyre?"

"Of course; that was all settled before."

"You are not, perhaps, aware that I was christened St John Eyre Rivers?"

"No, indeed! But what then? Surely—"

I stopped. I could not trust myself to entertain, much less to express, the thought that rushed upon me – that embodied itself – that, in a second, stood out a strong, solid probability.

"My mother's name was Eyre. She had two brothers: one a clergyman, who married Miss Jane Reed, of Gateshead; the other, John Eyre, merchant, late of Madeira. Mr Briggs, being Mr Eyre's solicitor, wrote to us last August to inform us of our uncle's death, and to say that he had left his property to his brother the clergyman's orphan daughter, overlooking us, in consequence of a quarrel, never forgiven, between him and my father. He wrote again a few weeks since, to intimate that the heiress was lost, and asking if we knew anything of her. A name casually written on a slip of paper has enabled me to find her out. You know the rest." Again, he was going, but I set my back against the door.

"Do let me speak," I said, "let me have one moment to draw breath and reflect." I paused—

# Chapter 33

"Your mother was my father's sister?"

"Yes."

"My aunt, consequently?"

He bowed.

"You three, then, are my cousins?"

"We are cousins, yes."

I surveyed him. This was wealth indeed – wealth to the heart! This was a blessing, bright, vivid, and exhilarating; not like the ponderous gift of gold, rich and welcome enough in its way, but sobering from its weight. I now clapped my hands in sudden joy.

"Oh, I am glad! I am glad!" I exclaimed.

St John smiled. "You were serious when I told you you had got a fortune and now, for a matter of no moment, you are excited."

"What can you mean? It may be of no moment to you – you have sisters – but I had nobody, and now three relations are born into my world!"

I walked fast through the room. I stopped, half suffocated with the thoughts that rose faster than I could comprehend them, thoughts of what might and should be. Those who had saved my life, I could now benefit. I could free them. They were scattered – I could reunite them. The independence which was mine, might be theirs too. Were we not four? Twenty thousand pounds shared equally would be five thousand each. It was a legacy of life, hope, enjoyment.

"Write to Diana and Mary to-morrow," I said, "and tell them to come home directly. Diana said they would both consider themselves rich with a thousand pounds, so with five thousand they will do very well. And what sort of an effect will the bequest have on you? Will it keep you in England, induce you to marry Miss Oliver, and settle down like an ordinary mortal?"

"You wander; your head becomes confused."

"Mr Rivers! I am rational enough. It is you who misunderstands."

"Perhaps, if you explained yourself a little more fully, I should comprehend better."

"What is there to explain? You cannot fail to see that twenty thousand pounds, divided equally between the nephew and three nieces of our uncle, will give five thousand to each? What I want is, that you should write to your sisters and tell them of the fortune that has accrued to them."

"To you, you mean."

"I have intimated my view of the case. I am incapable of taking any other. I am not selfish or ungrateful. Besides, I am resolved I will have a home and connections. It would please and benefit me to have five thousand pounds; it would torment and oppress me to have twenty thousand."

"You think so now," rejoined St John, "because you do not know what it is to possess, nor to enjoy wealth."

"And you," I interrupted, "cannot at all imagine the craving I have for fraternal and sisterly love. I never had a home, never had brothers or sisters."

"Jane, Jane, I will be your brother—my sisters will be your sisters—but, your aspirations after family ties may be realised otherwise: you may marry."

"I don't want to marry, and never shall marry."

"That is saying too much."

"It is not saying too much. No one would take me for love, and I will not be regarded in the light of mere money."

"And the school, Miss Eyre? It must now be shut up, I suppose?"

"No. I will retain my post of mistress till you get a substitute."

He smiled approbation. We shook hands, and he took leave.

I need not narrate in detail the further struggles I had to get matters regarding the legacy settled as I wished. My task was a very hard one, but as my cousins saw that my mind was really fixed on making a just division of the property, they yielded at length. The transfer was drawn out: St John, Diana, Mary, and I, each became possessed of a share.

# Chapter 34

It was near Christmas by the time all was settled; the season of general holiday approached. I now closed Morton school. Mr Rivers came up as having seen the classes, now numbering sixty girls, file out before me and locked the door, I stood with the key.

"Do you consider you have got your reward?" asked Mr Rivers, when they were gone. "And you have only toiled a few months! Would not a life devoted to the task be well spent?"

"Yes," I said, "but I could not go on for ever so. I want to enjoy my own faculties as well as to cultivate those of other people."

He looked grave. "What now? What are you going to do? What aim, what purpose, what ambition in life have you now?"

"My first aim will be to clean down Moor House from chamber to cellar. My purpose, in short, is to have all things in an absolutely perfect state of readiness for Diana and Mary before next Thursday when they come."

St John smiled slightly. Still he was dissatisfied.

"It is all very well for the present," said he, "but seriously, I trust that you will look a little higher than domestic endearments and household joys. Do not turn slothful."

I looked at him with surprise. "St John," I said, "I think you are almost wicked to talk so. I feel I have adequate cause to be happy, and I will be happy. Goodbye!"

Happy at Moor House I was, and hard I worked and so did Hannah. It was delightful by degrees to invoke order from the chaos. When all was finished, I thought Moor House a complete model of bright modest snugness. The eventful Thursday at length came and all was in readiness.

St John arrived first. He found me in the kitchen, and approaching the hearth, he asked, "If I was at last satisfied with housemaid's work?" I answered by inviting him to accompany me on a general inspection of my labours. I got him to make the tour, but not a syllable did he utter indicating pleasure in the improved aspect of his abode. This silence damped me.

I did not like this, reader. St John was a good man, but I began to feel he had spoken truth when he said he was hard and cold. He lived only to aspire after what was good and great, certainly, but he would never rest, nor approve of others resting round him. As I looked at his lofty forehead, still and pale as a white stone, I comprehended all at once that he would hardly make a good husband: that it would be a trying thing to be his wife. I saw he was too often cold, gloomy and out of place. "This parlour is not his sphere," I reflected. "He is right to choose a missionary's career. I see it now."

"They are coming! they are coming!" cried Hannah, throwing open the parlour door. Mary and Diana were delighted with the renovation and decorations of their rooms; with the new drapery, and fresh carpets, they expressed their gratification ungrudgingly. I had the pleasure of feeling that what I had done added to their joyous return home.

I am afraid the whole of the ensuing week tried St John's patience. St John did not rebuke our vivacity, but he escaped from it. He was seldom in the house. His parish was large, the population scattered, and he found daily business in visiting the sick and poor.

One morning at breakfast, Diana asked him, "If his plans were yet unchanged."

"Unchanged and unchangeable," was the reply. And that his departure from England was now definitively fixed for the ensuing year.

"And Rosamond Oliver?" suggested Mary.

"Rosamond Oliver," said he, "is about to be married to Mr Granby. I had the intelligence from her father yesterday."

His sisters looked at each other and at me. We all three looked at him. He was serene as glass.

# Chapter 34

St John had not kept his promise of treating me like his sisters. Now that I was acknowledged his kinswoman, and lived under the same roof with him, I felt the distance between us to be far greater than when he had known me only as the village schoolmistress.

As our mutual happiness (*i.e.*, Diana's, Mary's, and mine) settled into a quieter character, and we resumed our usual habits and studies, St John stayed more at home. While Mary drew, Diana pursued reading and I German, he pondered some Eastern tongue, the acquisition of which he thought necessary to his plans.

One afternoon, his sisters were gone to Morton and I sat reading German. I happened to look his way.

"Jane, what are you doing?"

"Learning German."

"I want you to give up German and learn Hindostanee."

He then went on to explain that Hindostanee was the language he was himself at present studying and that it would assist him greatly to have a pupil with whom he might go over the elements. Would I do him this favour? I should not, perhaps, have to make the sacrifice long, as it wanted now barely three months to his departure. St John was not a man to be lightly refused: I consented.

I found him a very patient, very forbearing, and yet an exacting master; he expected me to do a great deal. By degrees, he acquired a certain influence over me that took away my liberty of mind. I could no longer talk or laugh freely when he was by, because that vivacity was distasteful to him; only serious moods and occupations were acceptable. I fell under a freezing spell. When he said "go," I went; "come," I came; "do this," I did it. I daily wished more to please him, but to do so, I felt daily more and more that I must disown half my nature, stifle half my faculties, and force myself towards pursuits for which I had no natural vocation.

One evening when, at bedtime, his sisters and I stood round him bidding him good-night, he kissed them and, as was his custom, he gave me his hand. Diana, exclaimed –

"St John! You used to call Jane your third sister, but you don't treat her as such: you should kiss her too."

I felt uncomfortably confused when St John bent his head and kissed me. There are no such things as marble kisses or ice kisses, otherwise I should say my cousin's belonged to one of these classes. He never omitted the ceremony afterwards.

Perhaps you think I had forgotten Mr Rochester, reader, amidst these changes of place and fortune. Not for a moment. His idea was still with me, because it was a name graven on a tablet, fated to last as long as the marble it inscribed. I sought my bedroom each night to brood over it.

In the course of my correspondence with Mr Briggs about the will, I had inquired if he knew anything of Mr Rochester's present residence and state of health, but he was quite ignorant of all concerning him. I then wrote to Mrs Fairfax, entreating information on the subject. When two months wore away, and day after day the post brought nothing for me, I fell a prey to the keenest anxiety. I wrote again. When half a year wasted in vain expectancy, my hope died out, and then I felt dark indeed.

Diana tried to cheer me. She said I looked ill, and wished to accompany me to the sea-side. This St John opposed: he said I wanted employment; my present life was too purposeless; I required an aim, and to further my lessons in Hindostanee. I could not resist him.

One day I had come to my studies in lower spirits than usual. As I sat poring over the flourishing hand of an Indian scribe, my eyes filled with tears. St John and I were the only occupants of the parlour. My companion expressed no surprise at this emotion, nor did he question me as to its cause. He only said –

"Now, Jane, you shall take a walk and with me."

My present mood did not incline me to mutiny; I observed careful obedience to St John's directions and in ten minutes I was treading the wild track of the glen, side by side with him.

The breeze was from the west. It came over the hills, sweet with scents of heath and rush. The sky was of stainless blue; the stream descending the ravine, swelled with past spring rains, poured along plentiful and clear, catching golden gleams from the sun, and sapphire tints from the firmament. As we advanced and left the track, we trod a soft turf, mossy fine and emerald green, minutely enamelled with a tiny white flower, and spangled with a star-like yellow blossom. The hills, meantime, shut us quite in, for the glen, towards its head, wound to their very core.

"Let us rest here," said St John, as we reached the first stragglers of a battalion of rocks.

I took a seat. St John stood near me.

"Jane, I go in six weeks. I have taken my berth in an East Indiaman which sails on the 20th of June."

"God will protect you, for you have undertaken His work," I answered.

"Yes," said he, "there is my glory and joy. It seems strange to me that all round me do not burn to enlist under the same banner – to join in the same enterprise."

"All have not your powers. If they are really qualified for the task, will not their own hearts be the first to inform them of it?"

"And what does your heart say?" demanded St John.

"My heart is mute – my heart is mute," I answered.

"Then I must speak for it," continued the deep, relentless voice. "Jane, come with me to India; come as my helpmeet and fellow-labourer."

"Oh, St John!" I cried, "have some mercy!"

"God and nature intended you for a missionary's wife," he continued. "You are formed for labour, not for love. A missionary's wife you must – shall be. You shall be mine. I claim you – not for my pleasure, but for my Sovereign's service."

"I am not fit for it. I have no vocation," I said.

"I have watched you ever since we first met; I have made you my study for ten months. I have proved you in that time by sundry tests. And what have I seen? In the village school I found you could perform well, labour disagreeable to your inclinations. In the calm with which you learnt you had become suddenly rich, I read a mind clear of vice; in the tractability with which, at my wish, you forsook a study and adopted another because it interested me and which you have since persevered, I acknowledge the qualities I seek. Jane, you are docile, diligent, disinterested, faithful, constant, and courageous. As a conductress of Indian schools, and a helper amongst Indian women, your assistance will be to me invaluable."

My iron shroud contracted round me; persuasion advanced with slow sure step. He waited for an answer. I demanded a quarter of an hour to think, before I again hazarded a reply.

"I can do what he wants me to do. I am forced to see and acknowledge that," I meditated. "Of course I must seek another interest in life to replace the one lost. Is not the occupation he now offers me truly the most glorious man can adopt or God assign?"

"Consent, then, to his demand is possible, but for one item – one dreadful item. It is – that he asks me to be his wife and has no husband's heart for me. He prizes me as a soldier would a good weapon and that is all. Can I receive from him the bridal ring, endure all the forms of love (which I doubt not he would scrupulously observe) and know that the spirit was quite absent? No! Such a martyrdom would be monstrous. I will never undergo it. As his sister, I might accompany him – not as his wife. I will tell him so."

I looked towards the knoll. He started to his feet and approached me.

"I am ready to go to India, if I may go free. You have hitherto been my adopted brother – I, your adopted sister; let us continue as such. You and I had better not marry."

He shook his head. "If you were my real sister it would be different, but as it is, either our union must be consecrated by marriage, or it cannot exist. Do you not see it, Jane? I want a wife; the sole helpmeet I can influence efficiently in life, and retain absolutely till death."

I shuddered as he spoke. I felt his influence in my marrow – his hold on my limbs.

"Seek one elsewhere than in me, St John. Seek one fitted to you. Oh! I will give my heart to God," I said. "You do not want it."

## Chapter 34

I had silently feared St John till now, because I had not understood him, but revelations were being made in this conference. I understood that, sitting there where I did, on the bank of heath, and with that handsome form before me, I sat at the feet of a man, erring as I. Having felt in him the presence of these qualities, I felt his imperfection and took courage. I was with an equal – one with whom I might argue – one whom I might resist. He was silent after I had uttered the last sentence, and I presently risked an upward glance at his countenance.

"It is what I want," he said, speaking to himself, "it is just what I want. We must be married. I repeat it. There is no other way and undoubtedly enough of love would follow upon marriage."

"I scorn your idea of love," I could not help saying, as I rose up and stood before him. "I scorn the counterfeit sentiment you offer, St John, and I scorn you when you offer it."

He looked at me fixedly. "To-morrow," he said, "I leave home for Cambridge. I shall be absent a fortnight – take that space of time to consider my offer and do not forget that if you reject it, it is not me you deny, but God."

As I walked by his side homeward, I read well in his iron silence the disappointment of meeting resistance where he expected submission. In short, as a man, he would have wished to coerce me into obedience.

That night, after he had kissed his sisters, he thought proper to forget even to shake hands with me.

I ran after him.

"Good-night, St John," said I.

"Good-night, Jane," he replied calmly.

"Then shake hands," I added.

What a cold, loose touch he impressed on my fingers! When I asked him if he forgave me, he answered that he had nothing to forgive, not having been offended. And with that answer he left me. I would much rather he had knocked me down.

# Chapter 35

He did not leave for Cambridge the next day, as he had said he would. He deferred his departure a whole week, and during that time he made me feel what severe punishment a good yet stern, a conscientious yet implacable man can inflict on one who has offended him.

He had forgiven me for saying I scorned him and his love, but he had not forgotten the words and he never would forget them. They were always written on the air between me and him. To me, he was in reality become no longer flesh, but marble; his eye was a cold, bright, blue gem; his tongue a speaking instrument – nothing more.

All this was torture to me – refined, lingering torture. I felt how, if I were his wife, this good man, pure as the deep sunless source, could soon kill me, without drawing from my veins a single drop of blood, or receiving on his own crystal conscience the faintest stain of crime. To his sisters, meantime, he was somewhat kinder than usual. Afraid that mere coldness would not sufficiently convince me how completely I was banished and banned, he added the force of contrast.

The night before he left home, happening to see him walking in the garden about sunset, I was moved to make a last attempt to regain his friendship. I approached him as he stood leaning over the little gate.

"St John, I am unhappy because you are still angry with me. Let us be friends."

"Are we not? That is wrong. For my part, I wish you no ill and all good."

This, spoken in a cool, tranquil tone, was mortifying and baffling enough. I deeply venerated my cousin's talent and principle. His friendship was of value to me; to lose it tried me severely. I would attempt to reconquer it.

# Chapter 35

"Must we part in this way, St John? And when you go to India, will you leave me so, without a kinder word than you have yet spoken?"

He now turned quite from the moon and faced me.

"And you will not marry me?"

"No. St John, I will not marry you. I adhere to my resolution."

"Once more, why this refusal?" he asked.

"Formerly," I answered, "because you did not love me. Now, I reply, because you almost hate me. If I were to marry you, you would kill me. You are killing me now."

His lips and cheeks turned white – quite white.

"Now you will indeed hate me," I said. "It is useless to attempt to conciliate you. I see I have made an eternal enemy of you."

Most bitterly he smiled. "And now you recall your promise, and will not go to India at all, I presume?" said he, after a considerable pause.

"Yes, I will, as your assistant," I answered.

"I before proved to you the absurdity of the plan. Your own fortune will make you independent and thus you may still be spared the dishonour of breaking your promise and deserting the band you engaged to join."

Now I never had, as the reader knows, either given any formal promise or entered into any engagement, and this language was all much too hard and much too despotic for the occasion. I replied:

"There is no dishonour, no breach of promise, no desertion in the case. I am not under the slightest obligation to go to India. With you I would have ventured much, but I am convinced that I should not live long in that climate."

"Ah! You are afraid of yourself," he said, curling his lip.

"I am. God did not give me my life to throw away. Moreover, before I definitively resolve on quitting England there is a point on which I have long endured painful doubt, and I can go nowhere till by some means that doubt is removed."

"I know where your heart turns and to what it clings. Long since you ought to have crushed it. Now you should blush to allude to it. You think of Mr Rochester?"

It was true. I confessed it by silence.

"Are you going to seek Mr Rochester?"

"I must find out what is become of him."

"It remains for me, then," he said, "to remember you in my prayers, and to entreat God for you."

He opened the gate, passed through it, and strayed away down the glen. He was soon out of sight. On re-entering the parlour, I found Diana standing at the window, looking very thoughtful.

"Jane," she said, "tell me what business St John and you have on hands. That brother of mine cherishes peculiar views of some sort respecting you, I am sure. I wish he loved you – does he, Jane?"

"No, Diana, not one whit."

"Then why does he get you so frequently alone with him, and keep you so continually at his side? Mary and I had both concluded he wished you to marry him."

"He does – he has asked me to be his wife."

Diana clapped her hands. "That is just what we hoped and thought! And you will marry him, Jane, won't you? And then he will stay in England."

"Far from that, Diana. His sole idea in proposing to me is to procure a fitting fellow-labourer in his Indian toils."

"Madness!" she exclaimed. "You would not live three months there, I am certain. You never shall go. You have not consented, have you, Jane?"

"I have refused to marry him—"

"And have consequently displeased him?" she suggested.

"Deeply. He will never forgive me, I fear. Would it not be strange, Diana, to be chained for life to a man who regarded one but as a useful tool?"

# Chapter 35

"Insupportable – unnatural – out of the question! And yet St John is a good man," said Diana.

"He is a good and a great man, but he forgets the feelings of little people, in pursuing his own large views. Here he comes! I will leave you, Diana." And I hastened upstairs as I saw him entering the garden.

But I was forced to meet him again at supper. And for the evening reading before prayers he selected the twenty-first chapter of Revelation.

"He that overcometh shall inherit all things and I will be his God, and he shall be my son. But," was slowly, distinctly read, "the fearful, the unbelieving, shall have their part in the lake which burneth with fire and brimstone, which is the second death."

Henceforward, I knew what fate St John feared for me. In the prayer following, he supplicated strength for the weak-hearted, guidance for wanderers from the fold; a return, even at the eleventh hour, for those whom the temptations of the world and the flesh were luring from the narrow path. The prayer over, we took leave of him. He was to go at a very early hour in the morning. I tendered my hand and wished him a pleasant journey.

"Thank you, Jane. I shall return from Cambridge in a fortnight. That space, then, is yet left you for reflection. If I listened to human pride, I should say no more to you of marriage with me, but I listen to my duty, and keep steadily in view my first aim – to do all things to the glory of God."

He laid his hand on my head as he uttered the words. He had spoken earnestly, mildly. His look was not, indeed, that of a lover beholding his mistress, but it was that of a pastor recalling his wandering sheep – or of a guardian angel watching the soul for which he is responsible. I felt veneration for St John. I was tempted to cease struggling with him – to rush down the torrent of his will into the gulf of his existence, and there lose my own.

I stood motionless under his touch. My refusals were forgotten – my fears overcome – my wrestlings paralysed. The Impossible – that is, my marriage with St John – was fast becoming the Possible. Religion called – Angels beckoned – God commanded.

"Could you decide now?" asked the missionary. The inquiry was put in gentle tones; he drew me to him as gently. Oh, that gentleness! How far more potent is it than force! I grew pliant as a reed under his kindness.

"I could decide if I were but certain," I answered, "were I but convinced that it is God's will I should marry you, I could vow to marry you here and now – come afterwards what would!"

"My prayers are heard!" exclaimed St John. He surrounded me with his arm, almost as if he loved me.

"Show me, show me the path!" I entreated of Heaven.

All the house was still. The one candle was dying out; the room was full of moonlight. My heart beat fast and thick. Suddenly it stood still to an inexpressible feeling as sharp, as strange, as startling as an electric shock. It acted on my senses as if they were now summoned and forced to wake. They rose expectant. Eye and ear waited while the flesh quivered on my bones.

"What have you heard? What do you see?" asked St John. I saw nothing, but I heard a voice somewhere cry –

"Jane! Jane! Jane!" – nothing more.

"O God! What is it?" I gasped.

It did not seem in the room – nor in the house – nor in the garden. It did not come out of the air – nor from under the earth – nor from overhead. I had heard it; it was the voice of a human being – a known, loved, well-remembered voice – that of Edward Fairfax Rochester, and it spoke in pain and woe, wildly, eerily, urgently.

"I am coming!" I cried. "Wait for me! Oh, I will come!"

I flew to the door and ran out into the garden. It was void.

"Where are you?" I exclaimed.

The hills beyond Marsh Glen sent the answer faintly back – "Where are you?" I listened. The wind sighed low in the firs. All was moorland loneliness and midnight hush.

## Chapter 35

I broke from St John, who had followed, and would have detained me. It was my time to assume ascendency. My powers were in play and in force. I told him to forbear question or remark. I desired him to leave me; I must and would be alone. He obeyed at once. I mounted to my chamber, locked myself in, fell on my knees and prayed. My soul rushed out in gratitude; I rose from the thanksgiving and lay down, eager for daylight.

# Chapter 36

The daylight came. I rose at dawn. I busied myself for an hour or two with arranging my things in my chamber. Meantime, I heard St John quit his room. He stopped at my door: I feared he would knock – no, but a slip of paper was passed under the door. I took it up.

"You left me too suddenly last night. I shall expect your clear decision when I return this day fortnight. Meantime, watch and pray that you enter not into temptation; the spirit, I trust, is willing, but the flesh, I see, is weak. I shall pray for you. —Yours, ST JOHN."

"My spirit," I answered mentally, "is willing to do what is right, and my flesh is strong enough to accomplish the will of Heaven, when once that will is distinctly known to me."

It was yet two hours until breakfast-time. I filled the interval in walking softly about my room, and recalling that inward sensation I had experienced, for I could recall it, with all its unspeakable strangeness. I recalled the voice I had heard; it seemed in me – not in the external world. Was it a delusion? It was more like an inspiration.

At breakfast I announced to Diana and Mary that I was going on a journey, and should be absent at least four days. Diana asked me if I was sure I was well enough to travel. I looked very pale, she observed. I replied that nothing ailed me save anxiety of mind, which I hoped soon to alleviate.

I left Moor House at three o'clock, and soon after four I stood at the foot of the sign-post of Whitcross, waiting the arrival of the coach which was to take me to distant Thornfield. I heard it approach, the same vehicle whence, a year ago, I had alighted one summer evening on this very spot

## Chapter 36

– how desolate, and hopeless! Once more on the road to Thornfield, I felt like the messenger-pigeon flying home.

It was a journey of six-and-thirty hours. I had set out from Whitcross on a Tuesday afternoon, and early on the succeeding Thursday morning the coach stopped to water the horses at a wayside inn. I knew the character of this landscape. I was sure we were near my bourne.

"How far is Thornfield Hall from here?" I asked of the stablehand.

"Just two miles, ma'am, across the fields."

I got out of the coach, paid my fare and was going. The brightening day gleamed on the sign of the inn, and I read in gilt letters, "The Rochester Arms." My heart leapt up. I was already on my master's very lands. It fell again; the thought struck it:

"Your master himself may be beyond the British Channel, and then, if he is at Thornfield Hall, towards which you hasten, who besides him is there? His lunatic wife. You had better go no farther. Go up to the inn, and inquire if Mr Rochester be at home."

The suggestion was sensible, and yet I could not force myself to act on it. To prolong doubt was to prolong hope. How fast I walked! How I ran sometimes! At last the woods rose; on I hastened. Another field crossed – and there were the courtyard walls. "My first view of it shall be in front," I determined, "where I can single out my master's very window. Perhaps he will be standing at it!"

I had coasted along the lower wall of the orchard. There was a gate just there, and opening into the meadow I advanced my head with precaution. The crows sailing overhead perhaps watched me while I took this survey. I wonder what they thought. They must have considered I was very careful and timid at first, and that gradually I grew very bold and reckless. A peep, and then a long stare; and then straying out into the meadow and a sudden stop full in front of the great mansion, and a protracted, hardy gaze towards it. I looked with joy towards a stately house. I saw a blackened ruin.

No need to cower behind a gate-post, indeed! No need to listen for doors opening, to fancy steps on the pavement or the gravel-walk! The front was but a shell-like wall, very high and very fragile-looking. No roof, no chimneys – all had crashed in. And there was the silence of death about it. The grim blackness of the stones told how the Hall had fallen – by fire. But how kindled? What story belonged to this disaster? Had life been wrecked as well as property? If so, whose?

In wandering round the shattered walls and through the devastated interior, I gathered evidence that the calamity was not recent. Grass and weed grew here and there between the stones and fallen rafters. And oh! Where was the owner of this wreck? In what land?

Some answer must be had to these questions. I could find it nowhere but at the inn, and thither I returned. The host himself brought my breakfast into the parlour. I requested him to shut the door and sit down.

"You know Thornfield Hall, of course?" I managed to say at last.

"Yes, ma'am."

"Is Mr Rochester living at Thornfield Hall now?" I asked.

"No, ma'am – oh, no! No one is living there. I suppose you are a stranger in these parts, or you would have heard what happened last autumn. Thornfield Hall is quite a ruin: it was burnt down just about harvest-time. The fire broke out at dead of night. It was a terrible spectacle I witnessed it myself."

"At dead of night!" I muttered. Yes, that was ever the hour of fatality at Thornfield. "Was it known how it originated?" I demanded.

"They guessed, ma'am, they guessed. Indeed, I should say it was ascertained beyond a doubt. You are not perhaps aware," he continued, edging his chair a little nearer the table, and speaking low, "that there was a lady – a – a lunatic, kept in the house?"

"I have heard something of it."

"She was kept in very close confinement, ma'am. No one saw her. They said Mr Edward had brought her from abroad, and some believed she had been his mistress. This lady, ma'am, turned out to be Mr Rochester's wife! The discovery was brought about in the strangest way. There was a young lady, a governess at the Hall, that Mr Rochester fell in—"

## Chapter 36

"But the fire," I suggested.

"I'm coming to that, ma'am – that Mr Edward fell in love with. The servants say they never saw anybody so much in love as he was. She was a little small thing, they say, almost like a child. I never saw her myself."

"You shall tell me this part of the story another time," I said, "but now I have a particular reason for wishing to hear all about the fire. Was it suspected that this lunatic, Mrs Rochester, had any hand in it?"

"You've hit it, ma'am. It's quite certain that it was her that set it going. She had a woman to take care of her called Mrs Poole. When Mrs Poole was fast asleep, the mad lady, who was as cunning as a witch, would take the keys out of her pocket and go roaming about the house. However, on this night, she set fire first to the hangings of the room next her own, and then she got down to a lower storey, and made her way to the chamber that had been the governess's. She kindled the bed there, but there was nobody sleeping in it, fortunately. The governess had run away two months before and for all Mr Rochester sought her as if she had been the most precious thing he had in the world, he never could hear a word of her, and he grew quite savage on his disappointment. He never was a wild man, but he got dangerous after he lost her. He would be alone, too. He sent Mrs Fairfax, the housekeeper, away. Miss Adèle, a ward he had, was put to school. He shut himself up like a hermit at the Hall."

"What! Did he not leave England?"

"Leave England? Bless you, no! He would not cross the door-stones of the house, except at night, when he walked just like a ghost about the grounds and in the orchard as if he had lost his senses."

"Then Mr Rochester was at home when the fire broke out?"

"Yes, indeed was he, and when all was burning, he got the servants out of their beds and helped them down himself, and went back to get his mad wife. And then they called out to him that she was on the roof, where she was standing, waving her arms, above the battlements, and shouting out till they could hear her a mile off. I saw her and heard her with my own eyes. She had long black hair; we could see it streaming against the flames as she stood. I witnessed, and several more witnessed, Mr Rochester ascend through the sky-light on to the roof. We heard him call 'Bertha!' We saw him approach her and then, ma'am, she yelled and gave a spring, and the next minute she lay smashed on the pavement."

"Dead?"

"Ay, dead."

"Good God!"

"You may well say so, ma'am. It was frightful!"

He shuddered.

"Were any other lives lost?"

"No – perhaps it would have been better if there had."

"What do you mean?"

"Poor Mr Edward!" he exclaimed. "He is alive, but many think he had better be dead."

"Why? How?" My blood was again running cold. "Where is he?" I demanded. "Is he in England?"

"Ay – ay – he's in England. He is stone-blind," he said at last. "Yes, he is stone-blind, is Mr Edward."

I summoned strength to ask what had caused this calamity.

"It was all his own courage. He wouldn't leave the house till everyone else was out before him. As he came down the great staircase at last, there was a great crash – all fell. He was taken out from under the ruins, alive, but sadly hurt. A beam had fallen in such a way as to protect him partly, but one eye was knocked out, and one hand so crushed that Mr Carter, the surgeon, had to amputate it directly. The other eye inflamed, and he lost the sight of that also. He is now helpless, indeed."

"Where is he? Where does he now live?"

"At Ferndean, a manor-house he has, about thirty miles off: quite a desolate spot."

"Who is with him?"

## Chapter 36

"Old John and his wife; he would have none else. He is quite broken down, they say."

"Let a carriage be got ready instantly, and if your post-boy can drive me to Ferndean before dark this day, I'll pay both you and him twice the hire you usually demand."

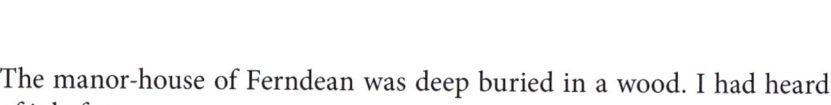

# Chapter 37

The manor-house of Ferndean was deep buried in a wood. I had heard of it before.

To this house I came on an evening marked by a sad sky and continued rain. The last mile I performed on foot, having dismissed the chaise and driver. Even when within a very short distance of the manor-house, you could see nothing of it, so thick and dark grew the gloomy wood about it. Iron gates showed me where to enter a grass-grown track which stretched on and on.

I proceeded. At last my way opened, and the trees thinned a little. Presently I beheld the house – scarce, by this dim light, distinguishable from the trees, so dank and green were its decaying walls. The windows were narrow; the front door was narrow too, one step led up to it. The whole looked, as the host of the Rochester Arms had said, "quite a desolate spot."

"Can there be life here?" I asked.

Yes, life of some kind there was, for I heard a movement – that narrow front-door was unclosing.

It opened slowly. A figure came out into the twilight and stood on the step. A man without a hat. He stretched forth his hand as if to feel whether it rained. Dusk as it was, I had recognised him – it was my master, Edward Fairfax Rochester, and no other.

I stayed my step, almost my breath, and stood to watch him. His form was of the same strong contour as ever: his hair was still raven black; nor were his features altered. But in his countenance I saw a change that looked desperate and brooding – that reminded me of some wronged wild beast, dangerous to approach.

## Chapter 37

He descended the one step, and advanced slowly and gropingly towards the grass-plat. Where was his daring stride now? Then he paused. He lifted his hand and opened his eyelids; gazed blank, and with a straining effort, on the sky: one saw that all to him was darkness. He groped his way back to the house, and, re-entering it, closed the door.

I now drew near and knocked. John's wife opened for me. "Mary," I said, "how are you?"

She started as if she had seen a ghost; I calmed her. To her hurried "Is it really you, miss, come at this late hour to this lonely place?" I answered by taking her hand, and then I followed her into the kitchen, where John now sat by a good fire. I explained to them, in few words, that I was come to see Mr Rochester. Just at this moment the parlour-bell rang.

"When you go in," said I, "tell your master that a person wishes to speak to him, but do not give my name."

"I don't think he will see you," she answered, "he refuses everybody."

When she returned, I inquired what he had said.

"You are to send in your name and your business," she replied. She then proceeded to fill a glass with water, and place it on a tray.

"Give the tray to me; I will carry it in."

I took it from her hand. She pointed me out the parlour door. The tray shook as I held it; my heart struck my ribs loud and fast.

This parlour looked gloomy. A neglected handful of fire burnt low in the grate and, leaning over it, appeared the tenant of the room. His old dog, Pilot, lay on one side and pricked up his ears when I came in, then jumped up and bounded towards me. Mr Rochester turned mechanically and sighed.

"Give me the water, Mary," he said.

Pilot followed me, still excited.

"Down, Pilot!" I again said.

"This is you, Mary, is it not?"

"Mary is in the kitchen," I answered.

He put out his hand with a quick gesture, but not seeing where I stood, he did not touch me. "Who is this?" he demanded. "Answer me – speak again!" he ordered.

"Pilot knows me," I answered.

"Great God! What delusion has come over me?"

"Your mind, sir, is too strong for delusion."

"And where is the speaker?"

He groped; I arrested his hand, and prisoned it in both mine.

"Her very fingers!" he cried. "If so there must be more of her."

My arm was seized, my shoulder – neck – waist – I was gathered to him.

"Is it Jane? This is her shape – this is her size—"

"And this her voice," I added. "She is all here, her heart, too."

"Jane Eyre! Jane Eyre!" was all he said.

"I am Jane Eyre," I answered. "I am come back to you."

"I cannot be so blest, after all my misery. It is a dream! Embrace me, Jane."

I pressed my lips to his once brilliant and now rayless eyes – I swept his hair from his brow, and kissed that too. He suddenly seemed to rouse himself.

"And you do not lie dead in some ditch under some stream? And you are not an outcast amongst strangers?"

"No, sir! I am an independent woman now."

"Independent! What do you mean, Jane?"

"My uncle in Madeira is dead, and he left me five thousand pounds."

"Ah! This is practical – this is real!" he cried: "I should never dream that. But as you are rich, Jane, you have now, no doubt, friends who will look after you, and not suffer you to burden yourself with me?"

# Chapter 37

"I told you I am independent, sir, as well as rich: I am my own mistress. I find you lonely; I will be your companion – to read to you, to walk with you, to be eyes and hands to you. You shall not be left desolate, so long as I live."

He replied not. He seemed serious. He sighed; he half-opened his lips as if to speak; he closed them again. I felt a little embarrassed. I had indeed made my proposal from the idea that he would ask me to be his wife, an expectation that he would claim me at once as his own. But I suddenly remembered that I might have been all wrong, and I began gently to withdraw myself from his arms – but he eagerly snatched me closer.

"No – no – Jane, you must not go. My very soul demands you."

"Well, sir, I will stay with you. I have said so."

"But you cannot always be my nurse, Jane: you are young – you must marry one day."

"I don't care about being married."

"You should care, Jane. if I were what I once was, I would try to make you care!"

He relapsed again into gloom. I, on the contrary, became more cheerful, and took fresh courage.

"Now, let me leave you an instant, to make a better fire, and have the hearth swept up?"

Summoning Mary, I soon had the room in more cheerful order. My spirits were excited, and with pleasure and ease I talked to him during supper, and for a long time after. There was no restraint, no repressing of glee with him; for with him I was at perfect ease, because I knew I suited him. All I said or did seemed either to console or revive him.

After supper, he began to ask me many questions: of where I had been, what I had been doing, how I had found him out.

"I have been with good people; far better than you."

"Who the deuce have you been with?"

"You shall not get it out of me to-night, sir, you must wait till to-morrow. To leave my tale half told will, you know, be a sort of security that I shall appear at your breakfast table to finish it. Now I'll leave you. I have been travelling these last three days, and I am tired. Good night."

"Just one word, Jane. Were there only ladies in the house where you have been?"

I laughed and made my escape, still laughing as I ran upstairs.

The next morning I came down as soon as I thought there was a prospect of breakfast. Entering the room very softly, I had a view of him before he discovered my presence. It was mournful, indeed, to witness how weakened was his spirit by bodily infirmity. I had meant to be gay and careless, but the powerlessness of the strong man touched my heart.

"It is a bright, sunny morning, sir," I said. "The rain is over and gone; you shall have a walk soon."

I had wakened the glow. His features beamed.

Most of the morning was spent in the open air. I led him out of the wet and wild wood into some cheerful fields. I described to him how brilliantly green they were, how sparklingly blue was the sky. I sought a seat for him in a hidden and lovely spot. Pilot lay beside us; all was quiet. He broke out suddenly while clasping me in his arms –

"Oh, Jane, what did I feel when I discovered you had fled from Thornfield and that you had taken no money, nor anything which could serve as an equivalent! What could my darling do, left penniless? And what did she do? Let me hear now."

Thus urged, I began the narrative of my experience for the last year.

I proceeded to tell him how I had been received at Moor House, and how I had obtained the office of schoolmistress. The accession of fortune, the discovery of my relations, followed in due order. Of course, St John Rivers' name came in frequently in the progress of my tale.

"This St John, then, is your cousin?"

"Yes."

## Chapter 37

"You have spoken of him often. Do you like him?"

"He was a very good man, sir. I could not help liking him."

"A good man. Does that mean a respectable well-conducted man of fifty? Or what does it mean?"

"St John was only twenty-nine, sir."

"And his brain? That is probably rather soft? He means well, but you shrug your shoulders to hear him talk?"

"He talks little, sir, but his brain is first-rate."

"Is he an able man, then?"

"St John is an accomplished and profound scholar."

"His appearance – I forget what description you gave of his appearance?"

"He is a handsome man – tall, fair, with blue eyes."

*(Aside.)* "Damn him!" – *(To me.)* "Did you like him, Jane?"

"Yes, Mr Rochester, I liked him, but you asked me that before."

I perceived, of course, that jealousy had got hold of him.

He paused. "St John made you schoolmistress of Morton before he knew you were his cousin?"

"Yes."

"You would often see him? He would visit the school sometimes?"

"Daily."

"How long did you reside with him and his sisters after the cousinship was discovered?"

"Five months."

"Did he study much?"

"A good deal."

"What?"

"Hindostanee."

"Did he teach you nothing?"

"A little Hindostanee."

"Rivers taught you Hindostanee?"

"Yes, sir."

"And his sisters also?"

"No."

"Only you?"

"Only me."

"Did you ask to learn?"

"No."

"He wished to teach you?"

"Yes."

A second pause.

"Why did he wish it? Of what use could Hindostanee be to you?"

"He intended me to go with him to India."

"Ah! He wanted you to marry him?"

"He asked me to marry him."

"That is a fiction – an impudent invention to vex me."

"I beg your pardon, it is the truth. He asked me more than once."

"Jane, your heart is not with me: it is with this cousin – this St John. Leave me. Go and marry Rivers."

"He will never be my husband. He does not love me; I do not love him. He wanted to marry me only because he thought I should make a suitable missionary's wife. He is good but severe, and cold as an iceberg."

I shuddered involuntarily. My master smiled.

## Chapter 37

"What, Jane! Is such really the state of matters between you and Rivers?"

"Absolutely, sir! Oh, you need not be jealous! All my heart is yours, sir. It belongs to you, and with you it would remain for ever."

He smiled.

"You speak of friends, Jane?" he asked.

"Yes, of friends," I answered rather hesitatingly.

"Ah! Jane. But I want a wife."

"Do you, sir?"

"Yes: is it news to you?"

"Of course: you said nothing about it before."

"Jane, will you marry me?"

"Yes, sir."

"Truly, Jane?"

"Most truly, sir."

"The case being so, we have nothing in the world to wait for; we must be married instantly."

He looked and spoke with eagerness. His old impetuosity was rising.

"Jane! you think me, I daresay, an irreligious dog, but my heart swells with gratitude to God just now. He sees not as man sees, but far clearer. Of late, Jane – only – only of late – I began sometimes to pray. Very brief prayers they were, but very sincere.

"Some days since, it was last Monday night, a singular mood came over me. I had long had the impression that since I could nowhere find you, you must be dead. Late that night I was in my own room, and sitting by the window, which was open. I longed for thee, Jane! I asked of God if I had not been long enough tormented. I pleaded, and my heart's wishes broke involuntarily from my lips in the words – 'Jane! Jane! Jane!'"

"Did you speak these words aloud?"

"I did, Jane. I pronounced them with such frantic energy."

"And it was last Monday night, somewhere near midnight?"

"Yes; but the time is of no consequence. What followed is the strange point. As I exclaimed 'Jane! Jane!' a voice – I cannot tell whence the voice came – replied, 'I am coming; wait for me.'"

Reader, it was on Monday night – near midnight – that I too had received the mysterious summons. Those were the very words by which I replied to it. I listened to Mr Rochester's narrative, but made no disclosure in return.

"I thank my Maker, that, in the midst of judgment, he has remembered mercy," he murmured as he rose.

Then he stretched his hand out to be led. I took that dear hand, held it a moment to my lips, then let it pass round my shoulder; being so much lower of stature than he, I served both for his prop and guide. We entered the wood, and wended homeward.

# Chapter 38

Reader, I married him. A quiet wedding we had. When we got back from church, I went into the kitchen of the manor-house, where Mary was cooking the dinner and John cleaning the knives, and I said –

"Mary, I have been married to Mr Rochester this morning." Mary looked up, and she stared at me. John, when I turned to him, was grinning from ear to ear.

"I telled Mary how it would be," he said: "I knew what Mr Edward would do and I was certain he would not wait long neither. And he's done right, for aught I know. I wish you joy, Miss!" and he politely pulled his forelock.

I wrote to Moor House and to Cambridge immediately to say what I had done, fully explaining also why I had thus acted. Diana and Mary approved the step unreservedly. Diana announced that she would just give me time to get over the honeymoon, and then she would come and see me.

How St John received the news, I don't know. He never answered the letter in which I communicated it, yet six months after, he wrote to me, without, however, mentioning Mr Rochester's name or alluding to my marriage. He has maintained a regular, though not frequent, correspondence ever since; he hopes I am happy, and trusts I am not of those who live without God in the world.

You have not quite forgotten little Adèle, have you, reader? I had not. I soon asked and obtained leave of Mr Rochester, to go and see her at the school where he had placed her. Her frantic joy at beholding me again moved me much. She looked pale and thin; she said she was not happy. I took her home with me and sought out a school conducted on a more indulgent system, and near enough to permit of my visiting her often, and bringing her home sometimes. As she grew up, I found in her a pleasing companion: good-tempered, and well-principled.

I have now been married ten years. I know what it is to live entirely for and with what I love best on earth. I hold myself supremely blest – blest beyond what language can express; because I am my husband's life as fully as he is mine.

Mr Rochester continued blind the first two years of our union. Perhaps it was that circumstance that drew us so very near – that knit us so very close, for I was then his vision, as I am still his right hand. He saw nature and he saw books through me, and never did I weary of gazing for his behalf. Never did I weary of reading to him; never did I weary of conducting him where he wished to go, of doing for him what he wished to be done.

One morning at the end of the two years, as I was writing a letter to his dictation, he came and bent over me, and said – "Jane, have you a glittering ornament round your neck?"

I had a gold watch-chain. I answered "Yes."

"And have you a pale blue dress on?"

I had. He informed me then, that for some time he had fancied the obscurity clouding one eye was becoming less dense and that now he was sure of it.

He eventually recovered the sight of that one eye. He cannot now see very distinctly; he cannot read or write much, but he can find his way without being led by the hand. The sky is no longer a blank to him – the earth no longer a void. When his first-born was put into his arms, he could see that the boy had inherited his own eyes, as they once were – large, brilliant, and black.

My Edward and I, then, are happy, and the more so, because those we most love are happy likewise. Diana and Mary Rivers are both married; alternately, once every year, they come to see us, and we go to see them.

As to St John Rivers, he left England: he went to India. He entered on the path he had marked for himself. He pursues it still. Firm, faithful, and devoted, full of energy, and truth, he labours for his race; he clears their painful way to improvement.

St John is unmarried. He never will marry now. His toil draws near its close; his glorious sun hastens to its setting. The last letter I received from him drew from my eyes human tears. He anticipated his sure reward. I know that a stranger's hand will write to me next, to say that the good and faithful servant has been called at length into the joy of his Lord. And why weep for this? No fear of death will darken St John's last hour. His own words are a pledge of this –

"My Master," he says, "has forewarned me. Daily He announces more distinctly, – 'Surely I come quickly!' and hourly I more eagerly respond, 'Amen; even so come, Lord Jesus!'"

The End

The accompanying Jane Eyre Abridged Teaching Resources are available for purchase at:

www.hachettelearning.com/english/jane-eyre-abridged-teaching-resources